Postcolonialism

Concepts in the Social Sciences

Series Editor: Frank Parkin

Published Titles

Concepts in the Social Sciences

Postcommunism

Richard Sakwa

Open University Press
Buckingham · Philadelphia

Open University Press
Celtic Court
22 Ballmoor
Buckingham
MK18 1XW

email: enquiries@openup.co.uk
world wide web: http://www.openup.co.uk

and
325 Chestnut Street
Philadelphia, PA 19106, USA

First Published 1999

A catalogue record of this book is available from the British Library

ISBN 0 335 20057 5 (pbk)   0 335 20058 3 (hbk)

Library of Congress Cataloging-in-Publication Data
Sakwa, Richard.
    Postcommunism / by Richard Sakwa.
        p.   cm. — (Concepts in the social sciences)
    Includes bibliographical references and index.
    ISBN 0-335-20058-3 (hbk)   ISBN 0-335-20057-5 (pbk)
    1. Communism.   2. Post-communism.   3. Capitalism.   I. Title.
II. Series
HX44.5.S25   1999
335.43—dc21   99-29821 CIP

Typeset by Type Study, Scarborough
Printed in Great Britain by The Cromwell Press, Trowbridge, Wiltshire

Contents

Introduction: Defining Postcommunism

Eric Hobsbawm described the 'short twentieth century' from 1914 to 1991 as 'the age of extremes'.[1] This was a period characterized by the struggle of ideologies, and in particular stamped by debates both within socialism and between various elements of the socialist tradition and its market-oriented alternatives, formalized after the Second World War in the geopolitical structures of the cold war. This age has apparently come to an end, but what comes next? The answer, it appears, is postcommunism, a term that is not restricted to countries where regimes once proclaimed themselves on the road to communism but one that has universal significance. It defines an epoch that claims to have moved beyond the 'extremism' of ideological politics and its associated 'metanarratives' towards a more open and 'discursive' type of politics.

Statement of the problem

According to Václav Havel, 'The fall of the Communist empire is an event on the same scale of historical importance as the fall of the Roman empire'.[2] Like the fall of great empires in the past, this particular 'dissolution of order', to use Arpád Szakolczai's term,[3] has both epochal and specific significance. If the coming to power of the Bolsheviks in Russia in October 1917 was the seminal event of the twentieth century, shaping the history of the following decades, then the fall of the regime was no less significant. In Jowitt's words, 'the Leninist extinction's impact will not be limited to the former communist world. Any argument that the collapse of Leninist regimes is some sort of historical surgical strike leaving the rest of the world largely unaffected qualifies as a striking example of political and intellectual denial.'[4] The fall of European communism in 1989–91 not only signified the end of the geopolitical confrontation between competing social systems, but also suggested the transcendence of the ideological conflict between socialism and capitalism. The ideological conflict had taken on the form of a confrontation between states in the years following the Bolshevik revolution but clearly had a dynamic that was separate from the fate of any particular country. The degree to which the Marxist critique of capitalism is invalidated because of the fall of the Soviet Union and its European allies is a theme we shall explore later, but for the present let us note that the strength of the revolutionary socialist challenge to capitalism did indeed derive much of its strength for the greater part of the twentieth century from the existence of a system operating in its name, and its fall radically undermined the force of the alternative.

The distinction is often drawn between communism as practised by some two dozen countries that proclaimed themselves on the road to communism, and an altogether purer theoretical form outlined by the founding fathers of the communist movement, Karl Marx, Frederick Engels and their successors. The distinction between the two communisms – the latter sometimes designated as 'Communism', while the former is more modestly referred to as 'communism' – is one that came to be accepted by communist leaders themselves. The emergence in the 1970s of the concept of 'actually existing socialism' (occasionally referred to as 'really existing socialism') appeared to signal a recognition by communist leaders that the version of communism that they had so assiduously developed diverged in important respects from the Communism that had once appeared possible. From the time of Nikita Khrushchev's revised Party Programme of 1961 communism appeared to shrink to become little more than an overblown version of the welfare states of Western Europe. It is not surprising that notions of convergence between East and West became current at this time, most forcefully in Daniel Bell's *The End of Ideology* (1960). Of human emancipation from the thrall of necessity, the core of Marx's revolutionary socialism, little remained in the ideology of late communism.

Just as there were two communisms, the 'actually existing' variety and the emancipatory view, so, too, we can identify two major strains of postcommunism. Postcommunism can refer either specifically to the 27 countries in Eurasia that at some point were part of the post-war communist order,[5] together with Mongolia and the Asian and Caribbean states that are in various stages of abandoning communism (China, Vietnam, Laos, North Korea and Cuba), or more broadly to the global post-socialist epoch inaugurated by the fall of the state socialist regimes in 1989–91. When used in the latter sense, postcommunism becomes a universal syndrome affecting all countries, irrespective of whether they were once communist. Thus postcommunism has both a universal and a specific meaning. In the universal sense, postcommunism suggests that the fall of the communist regimes changed the political and political-philosophical terrain not just in the countries directly affected but everywhere else as well – we are, from this perspective, all postcommunists now. Postcommunism becomes an important facet of global politics and social theory at the turn of the millennium. In its specific sense, postcommunism defines the challenges facing 33 countries, including the world's largest (Russia) and most populous (China). The relationship between the two types of postcommunism, as between the two types of communism earlier, is one of the most intriguing facing the political theorist.

We shall use the term in both senses. Postcommunism is by definition a negative concept, defining the present in terms of its past. In its universal sense it is in keeping with the nostalgic post-everything tenor of our times: we have done with modernity, moved out of the industrial age, possibly dispensed with materialism and the economy altogether and certainly moved beyond Fordism. The notion of postcommunism thus joins a large and expanding family of terms that appears to be no more than one syndrome among many others of a civilizational trajectory inaugurated by the Enlightenment that has turned full circle and is now in its declining stages. The politics of postism deserves separate treatment, but in our account we shall encounter many examples of the species, in particular postmodernism.

Historical and philosophical context

When applied in its more restricted specific sense, we are immediately faced with a problem: how can we talk in a systematic way of a reality that is constantly changing and of societies in a state of dynamic flux? Is there, indeed, something that we can define as 'postcommunism'? Is there anything that unites the countries in question other than their former communism? Similar issues are raised by a series of other 'post' states of the twentieth century: the post-imperial states following the disintegration of the empires after the First World War; the post-war societies after 1945; and the post-colonial countries after the dismantling of the European overseas empires after the Second World War.

The feature common to all of these is that they are post-crisis countries, societies that have rapidly changed from one condition to another. They are in a 'genesis environment', otherwise characterized as being in a state of 'liminality'.[6] In these states old orders have dissolved and the new ones are in flux where the basic contours of civilizational identity are contested and where there are conflicts over the fundamental issues of how power is to be legitimated, structured and applied. Post-colonialism, for example, is a discrete phenomenon, marking a distinct stage in the evolution of not only the objects of colonialism – of empire – but also of the former imperialists themselves. While post-colonial countries differ from region to region, and between individual countries, their 'post-colonial' status casts a long shadow over their domestic and international policies. For 'post' states the rejection of the past cannot but inhibit the open-endedness of future evolution. Coming to terms with the past, as we shall see, is one of the central features of postcommunism.

The postcommunist syndrome clearly has a commonality with post-fascism: a long emergency followed by the reconstruction of political order and the reformulation of political identities on a radically new basis. The commonalities are, however, deeper, since both fascism and communism were responses to similar problems – in particular, the challenge of state formation and the threats posed by modernity's dissolution of the bonds of tradition. Italy was only created as a state in the second half of the nineteenth century, and there remain profound difficulties in forging a nation-state. The problem of state formation in Germany is a special topic in itself, while Japan's reformulation as a modern nation-state was accompanied by a radical modernization that seemed to finesse the challenge posed by modernity. The problem of state formation in Russia remains acute, and its development as a nation-state remains profoundly ambiguous (quite apart from the notion itself being almost untranslatable). In China, too, the issue of state coherence in the transition has limited the options of the élite: democracy, it appears, is too high a price to pay for the loss of Tibet and the possible loosening of links with areas like Xinjiang.

Narrowly defined, postcommunism is characterized by the following features:

- The end of the communist party's monopoly over politics, economics and society.
- The emergence of pluralistic societies but ones where interests are weakly defined and where the establishment of genuine polyarchy (defined by Robert Dahl as competing sources of social power) is usually poorly institutionalized. The most vivid manifestation of this is the difficulty in establishing genuine multiparty pluralism.
- The uneven introduction of elements of the market into a heavily bureaucratized economy, facilitating rent-seeking and encouraging the corruption of economic relationships.
- The liberalization of prices accompanied by the retention of monopolistic concerns, a combination that provoked inflation, especially in the early phase of liberalization.
- Rapid changes in the class structure, with the emergence of a thoroughly monetized 'new' class enjoying its new-found wealth, often as a result of the leverage it exerted from being part of what Milovan Djilas had originally called the 'new class' of a communist officialdom enjoying the privileges derived from the management of state property.
- Equally rapid changes in the employment structure, above all marked by the shift from the manufacturing and industrial sectors to the service sector.
- The radical reorientation of foreign and, typically, security policy.
- The incomplete nature of the transformations, marked by the strong institutional, cultural and social imprint of the state socialist period on the postcommunist order. Continuity is particularly marked in the sphere of élite politics.
- The proliferation of new institutions and practices, often hybrids of the old yet oriented to very different purposes, although their *modus operandi* is often reminiscent of the past.

- The weakness of state capacity, including tax-raising ability.
- Tension between those who seek to draw a 'thick line' under the past, and those who believe that the perpetrators of communist violence should be brought to book.
- A generalized belief that autarchic development strategies are no longer viable and that the only option is to enter the global economy.
- Various facets of identity politics, including national, ethnic and cultural questions accompanied by the tension between 'nativist' trends and 'cosmopolitans' who define the transition in terms of 'rejoining world civilization'.

These issues are useful as a starting point, but fail to engage with the profound ambiguities of the whole phenomenon of societies moving away from one particular form of social order, which has resonances with pre-modern, traditional and patrimonial societies, to a new type of social order which is itself in profound crisis. Neither does it engage with the larger problem of the universal aspects of postcommunism, the challenge of devising a language of politics and alternatives once the old antinomies of capital and class have apparently been transcended. There are certainly teleological elements in the whole notion of postcommunism, but there is more to it than an updated version of the old modernization argument of linear developmental paths or of the contemporary democratization transition debate.

The enormous scope of the postcommunist project is staggering, with nearly three dozen countries fundamentally changing their entire orientations. The reform process itself generated new phenomena that raise questions about the received wisdom of the political sciences and economics. Although significant residues of the past remain, the scope of transformation has been unprecedented: monolithic societies are being converted into pluralistic ones, economies are being reoriented towards the market, new nations are being born, and states are rejoining the international community that is itself being recast. While analysis of postcommunism is inevitably focused on the former communist states, the wider international and ideological relevance of the phenomenon should not be neglected. The collapse of the Soviet bloc appeared to signal the onset of Western liberal capitalist global hegemony, despite the internal difficulties of the transitional states. We shall focus on the permanent, rather than the short-term, effects of the collapse of communism. Like Jean François Lyotard's definition of postmodernism – no centres, no metanarratives[7] – so, too, post-communism is a multi-faceted, heterogeneous phenomenon shot through with paradoxes while at the same time revealing the under-lying paradigmatic shifts, not only in theory but also in reality, of our times.

The Long Transcendence

No sooner did communism form as a relatively defined programme and body of thought than its *alter ego* and ultimate nemesis, postcommunism, emerged to haunt its 150-year-long trajectory. The spectre of Communism itself had a spectre – that of postcommunism. In this context postcommunism means the sustained philosophical and political repudiation of the basic postulates around which Marx and Engels formulated their concept of revolutionary socialism from within the socialist tradition. This is not to minimize the importance of non-socialist critiques of revolutionary socialism, but to suggest that they belong to a different analytical category – the repudiation of revolutionary socialism and not its immanent transcendence.

The road to postcommunism – reformist revisionism

The communist project as formulated in *The Communist Manifesto* (1848) of Marx and Engels was riven by a fundamental ambiguity from the very first. As Neil Harding formulates it:

> how could two bourgeois intellectuals manage to arrive at a know-ledge of the past, present and future of the working-class movement that was superior in every respect to the knowledge of the working class itself? How had two bourgeois intellectuals who had, moreover, framed a general sociology of knowledge in terms of which social situation was held to determine individual consciousness, themselves emerge as the most conspicuous exceptions to their own general rule?[1]

While the concept of the party was incipient in the *Manifesto*, it was Lenin who gave proletarian organization its modern institutional form, outlined theoretically in his *What is To Be Done?* (1902). The ambiguities suggested above were not resolved but were simply turned inwards, towards the leadership itself. The relation between the party that understood 'the line of march' and the working class that it claimed not so much to represent as to embody was deproblematized in Lenin's thinking. By claiming to know better the true interests of the working class than the working class itself, Leninism represented the *intellectual* marginalization of the class, a process that after 1917 resulted in its *political* expropriation. Communism became whatever Lenin – or Stalin – said it was. It is out of ambiguities like these that postcommunism was born. There were two main types of transcendence of the Marxian revolutionary socialist tradition – reformist revisionism and revolutionary revisionism. We cannot provide a full description of the development of either evolutionary socialist thinking or of what would later be described as anti-Bolshevik communism, but simply indicate some of the main themes.

It is usual to distinguish between Communism and socialism, with Marx, for example, in his *Critique of the Gotha Programme* (1875) suggesting that socialism was a lower stage in the transition towards Communism. Much earlier, in *The German Ideology* (1846), Marx and Engels had already blurred any strict distinction between Communism as the end state and socialism as a process: 'Communism is for us not a stable state which is to be established, an *ideal* to which reality will have to adjust itself. We call communism the *real* movement which abolishes the present state of things.'[2] The whole history of the twentieth century confirms that it is impossible to make a categorical distinction between the two – they are best seen as points along a shifting evolutionary continuum. There is, certainly, a great practical difference between revolutionary socialism and what later developed as evolutionary (or democratic) socialism, a difference that Lenin sought to encapsulate in the '21 conditions' for membership of the Comintern (Third International) formulated in 1920, but when we move from the realm of organization to theory the edges become blurred.

Evolutionary socialism as it evolved into social democracy was never quite sure whether it wanted to destroy capitalism or simply to civilize it, to restrain its excesses and remedy some of its distributional problems. Communism at least knew what it wanted – the destruction of capitalism – or at least it thought it did. Destroy the market by all means, comrades, but what did Marx really mean by using the achievements of capitalism as the foundation of communism? What did transcendence (*Aufhebung*) entail? How much should be saved and how much destroyed? And as for the achievements of 'bourgeois democracy', if bourgeois law and civil society were no more than a mask for capitalist exploitation, as Marx suggested in *On the Jewish Question* (1844), then what precisely were these 'achievements'? It is out of these ambiguities that the critique of communism from within the revolutionary movement itself emerged. Glimpses of postcommunism appeared at the precise time that communism itself emerged as a coherent ideology advocating the radical transformation of capitalist society. What begins as a purely intellectual challenge often becomes woven into the very fabric of life. It was 70 years after the publication of the *Communist Manifesto* that the Bolsheviks came to power in Russia. Similarly, the critiques of communism after a long gestation burst out in the form of postcommunism, and were similarly transformed by contact with reality.

Marxism is a theory of socialism based on the transcendence of liberalism and capitalism through revolution, but this theory was itself transcended. There were numerous milestones in the development of the reformist revisionist strand in universalistic postcommunism. Eduard Bernstein was the first of these 'spectres of the spectre', the ghost at the feast of the Second International established in 1889. In Bismarck's Germany universal suffrage was granted before the establishment of parliamentary government, allowing the Social Democratic Party (SPD) to emerge as the largest and most influential party in the Second International. Its Erfurt programme of 1891 was riven by tensions, propounding a catastrophist view of capitalism's inevitable demise accompanied by the pauperization of the working class. Bernstein, one of the leading figures in the SPD, shifted the critique to challenge the very theoretical basis of revolutionary socialism. In his best-known work, known in English as *Evolutionary Socialism* (1899), he revised basic features of classical Marxist theory: capitalist production would not inevitably break down but its increasing sophistication would allow it to avoid a terminal crisis; the class structure of capitalist society was not becoming increasingly polarized but in fact a middle class was growing to bridge the gulf between the owners and the proletariat; the sharpness of class antagonisms were therefore decreasing; thus there was no longer any need for a socialist revolution. Capitalism in his view was evolving into a system of rational social production, marked above all by the growth in the banking sector. The very basis of socialism shifted from an alleged scientific analysis of the system's inherent contradictions accompanied by class war to a Kantian ethical category of social justice. His analysis was prompted by the clear-sighted perception that the gulf between the SPD's revolutionary rhetoric and its reformist practices had to be overcome by a revision of the theory itself. Above all, the tension between the ultimate revolutionary goal of the movement and its reformist practices could be reconciled, in his view, only by repudiating the goal itself. As he put it in his famous statement:

> I frankly admit that I have extraordinarily little feeling for, or interest in, what is usually termed 'the final goal of socialism'. This goal, whatever it may be, is nothing to me, the movement is everything. And by movement I mean both the general movement of society, and the political and economic agitation and organisation to bring about this progress.[3]

While Bernstein's thinking lacked rigour and it appears that he misunderstood some key elements of Marx's thinking, his model of evolutionary socialism transcended the sterility of revolutionism as a political programme and sought a reconciliation of socialist and liberal thinking that prefigured the reform communists and Eurocommunists two generations later, when issues of democracy, political morality and human rights came to the fore. Bernstein unfortunately failed to systematize his model of evolutionary democratic socialism and thus his views, however prescient they may have been, were unable to sustain a coherent alternative either to orthodox Marxism or to uncritical liberalism. Bernstein's 'third way', like so many of the genre, proved an uncomfortable combination of incompatible elements from the other two and thus failed to transcend either.

Karl Kautsky, considered the most important theoretician of German social democracy, understood how progressive capital formation and improved labour conditions and wages, in Paul Mattick's words, objectively 'transformed the workers' struggle into a force for capitalist expansion'. Ironically, '[t]he more the workers gained, the richer capital became'; the greater the successes of the labour movement, the more they became 'steps towards its own destruction, creat[ing] a non-revolutionary ideology . . . However, this 'betrayal' did not very much bother those who were betrayed'.[4] This is the central theme of Donald Sassoon's *One Hundred Years of Socialism*.[5] For Kautsky there was nothing inherent about capitalism that required its violent overthrow since legal and peaceful means could, depending on circumstances, be used to achieve the transition to socialism, and thus Marx's devastatingly ill-defined concept of 'the dictatorship of the proletariat' could take parliamentary forms.

In his *The Day after the Revolution* (1902) Kautsky examined the problem of how a state bent on socialization would organize production, and rejected attempts to distribute goods 'barrack-fashion' as representing a retrograde step. Elements of the market, wages and money would have to remain, while the socialist state would concern itself with the larger enterprises. Kautsky began a debate that continues to this day: just how would socialism manage the economy in practice? How would prices be set in a socialist economy? This was a discussion that from the 1920s to the 1940s would be joined by Ludwig von Mises, Friedrich von Hayek, Oskar Lange and others when it was known as the 'calculation debate'; and by Ota Sik, Alec Nove and Włodimierz Brus from the 1960s when the issue focused on reform of the socialist economies and ways of overcoming their wastefulness and 'democratic deficit'.

At the heart of reformist revisionism was the rejection of the view that the abolition of the private ownership of the means of production – in effect, of market capitalism itself – was the road to socialism. By the 1950s almost all the Western socialist parties had rejected this fundamental Marxist postulate. For the SPD the fateful step was taken at the Bad Godesberg Congress in November 1959, making no mention of Marx, accepting the market and growth, but above all merging 'the party's immediate demands and its long-term aims', thus removing the contradiction that had haunted social democracy between short-term reformism and end-of-the-rainbow revolutionism.[6] In Britain Anthony Crosland distanced the Labour Party from Marxism,[7] although it was only under Tony Blair in 1994 that it dropped its commitment (Clause 4 of the 1918 programme) to the nationalization of the 'commanding heights' of the economy. Until the 1990s democratic socialism was on the agenda, although how this was to be defined remained unclear and socialism increasingly came to be seen as a set of progressive values devoid of a conception of an end state. These values focused on social equality, redistributive tax policies, extended welfarism and the Keynesian regulation of the economy for social ends. After 1989 even this residual commitment to socialism withered away. We shall return to the dilemmas of socialism after communism in Chapter 6.

The road to postcommunism – revolutionary revisionism

Mikhail Bakunin was the first to subject Marx's revolutionism to a critique from the revolutionary perspective itself. His critique from an anarchist revolutionary perspective focused on organizational issues and raised questions that would be echoed by revolutionary revisionists later. In his *Statism and Anarchy* (1873) he stated the problem succinctly:

> This means that no state, however democratic its forms, not even the *reddest* political republic . . . is capable of giving the people what they need: the free organization of their own interests from below upward, without any interference, tutelage, or coercion from above. That is because no state . . . in essence represents anything but government of the masses from above downward, by an educated and thereby privileged minority which supposedly understands the real interests of the people better than the people themselves.[8]

Marx's conception of the revolutionary state, in Bakunin's view, would simply lead to the 'reign of scientific intelligence, the most aristocratic, despotic, arrogant and contemptuous of all regimes'. According to Robin Blackburn, Bakunin's criticisms provoked Marx to reject the statism at the heart of German social democracy, epitomized by Ferdinand Lassalle's idea of the *Volksstaat*, in his *Critique of the Gotha Programme*.[9] Marx never resolved the problem of the state, both wanting one (his economic model of socialism was thoroughly statist) and wanting to see 'restored to the social body all the forces hitherto absorbed by the state parasite feeding upon, and clogging the free movement of society', as he put it in his idealized description of the Paris Commune of 1871.[10] His vision of commune democracy suggested a thoroughly decentralized self-managing model of politics, but how the economic life of the community would be run was left vague.

The Bolshevik seizure of power in October 1917 provoked a

storm of criticism that reached into the Bolshevik party itself. The coalitionists, for example, in the first weeks after the revolution insisted on the need for a broader socialist government, not only for practical reasons but also out of a principled fear that one-party rule would provoke civil war and lead to a dictatorship. Lenin faced down wave after wave of intra-party resistance to his style of rule – the Left Communists, the Democratic Centralists, the Workers' Opposition being only the best known – while at Kronstadt in March 1921 the working class rose up under the slogan of 'soviets without Bolsheviks'. Lenin's genius was not only to strike at the precise moment when the revolutionary seizure of power was possible, but also to forge a 'Leninist' regime out of the Marxist-Bolshevik tradition itself. Like Marx, however, Lenin paid little attention to the political institutions of socialism and tended towards a class reductionist understanding of organizations: for him the key issue was the social origin of those who staffed them rather than how they worked in practice. Above all, Lenin was unable to distinguish between opposition *to* the revolution from opposition *within* the revolution.[11] This led him to issue the 'ban on factions' in March 1921 that stifled the remnants of intra-party democracy.[12] The transformation of revolutionary socialist theory into a coercive dictatorship is not simply one of the problems of Soviet communism: it is *the* problem of Soviet-type systems.

One of the first foreign socialists to comment on the Bolshevik revolution was Rosa Luxemburg, characterized by Farber as a 'revolutionary revisionist'[13] even though she dedicated her life to the struggle against the revisionist notion that 'capitalist accumulation has no economic limit'.[14] Born in Poland, from 1900 Luxemburg focused her activities on the SPD and later helped establish the radical Spartacus League, which became the core of the German Communist Party in 1919. The Spartacist uprising in the first days of 1919 was crushed, and its leaders, Karl Liebknecht and Luxemburg, were murdered by reactionary officers 'while taking them to prison' on 16 January 1919. While welcoming Lenin's achievement in having 'put socialism on the order of the day', Luxemburg warned that Lenin's methods would undermine the purpose of socialism. For her, socialism was inseparable from democracy, remaining to the end of her life an ardent believer in the creative capacity of humanity. Socialism, as she saw it, was to extend democracy beyond the limits imposed by bourgeois capitalist rule, not to eliminate even that limited democracy. While not flinching from violence, she regarded the dictatorial elements as temporary and to be balanced by the extension of democracy:

> Lenin says: the bourgeois state is an instrument of oppression of the working class; the socialist state, of the bourgeoisie. To a certain extent, he says, it is only the capitalist state stood on its head. This simplified view misses the most essential thing: bourgeois class rule has no need of the political training and education of the entire mass of the people, at least not beyond certain narrow limits. But for the proletarian dictatorship that is the life element, the very air without which it is not able to exist . . .[15]

No party, for her, had a monopoly on wisdom: a revolution was to reflect the free spontaneous creativity of the masses. All this was a far cry from Lenin's dictatorship.

Kautsky had been one of Bernstein's fiercest critics, yet following the Bolshevik seizure of power in October 1917 he found himself in profound opposition to the new regime. He took up the theme of democracy in his pamphlet *The Dictatorship of the Proletariat* (1918), arguing that Marx's notion of the 'dictatorship of the proletariat' had been intended as a social category rather than as a political form of rule and thus he defended parliamentarianism as an essential part of the socialist programme. He insisted that democracy was more than an instrument in the struggle for power, but an essential part of socialism itself:

> For us, therefore, Socialism without democracy is unthinkable. We understand by Modern Socialism not merely social organisation of production, but democratic organisation of society as well. Accordingly, Socialism is for us inseparably connected with democracy. No Socialism without democracy . . . A government so strongly supported by the masses has not the least occasion to interfere with democracy . . . But a government which knows that the masses are behind it would only use force to protect democracy, and not to subvert it. It would be committing suicide to cast aside such a strong support as universal suffrage, which is a powerful source of moral authority.[16]

The work marked an important stage in the division between social democracy and communism. He considered the Russian revolution not part of a broader anti-capitalist movement but a result of exceptional circumstances born of war and Russian conditions; Lenin's dictatorship, Kautsky insisted, would in fact impede the move towards socialism. The Bolshevik revolution was thus deprived of a universal significance; this in part explains Lenin's vitriolic response in *The Proletarian Revolution and the Renegade Kautsky* (1919), but the storm of invective was in part designed to cover his lack of an answer to Kautsky's arguments.

By the time of the Third International all the ghosts appeared to have been exorcized from within the movement, and yet even here 'revisionism' in the form of Antonio Gramsci's views on hegemony and civil society took root. Gramsci's great achievement was to reappropriate into socialist discourse the concept of civil society as more than the arena for capitalist exploitation but as a sphere of political action. Although Gramsci remained locked into a revolutionary way of thinking, his sophisticated analysis of various forms of political action, including the 'passive revolution' of coopting an opponent's best ideas, marks him out as a thinker of great originality in conceptualizing the way that socialism could transcend capitalism. Ironically, his thinking was ultimately appropriated most effectively as a strategy to transcend revolutionary socialism itself.

Hegel's distinction between the state and civil society characterized the latter as plagued by sectional interests that could only be reconciled in the universal state. Marx rejected any notion of a 'universal' state – for him the state could only be an instrument of class oppression, while he debased civil society into little more than the realm of market relations. Marx collapsed the complex institutions of modern society into the exploitative relations of a mode of production. The long struggle for individual autonomy (exemplified by habeas corpus) and civil association was discounted. It was Gramsci who insisted that civil society was a sphere of social relations distinct *both* from the state and from the economy. Thus the struggle for hegemony in civil society could be used by socialists against the state, an insight that was used by oppositional movements *against* communism later, particularly in Poland (see below).

Nikolai Bukharin had sparred with Lenin during the First World War over the repressive potential of the modern state, and in the spring of 1918 he became the best-known of the Left Communists. In place of Lenin's view on the need to accept the harsh terms of the Treaty of Brest-Litovsk ceding large areas of Russia to Germany, Bukharin advocated revolutionary war; and instead of Lenin's 'state capitalism', he called for worker self-management. By the 1920s, however, he had become a 'Rightist', advocating a ride to socialism 'on the peasant nag'. According to Stephen Cohen, Bukharin represented a viable alternative to Stalin based on the relative moderation of the New Economic Policy.[17] Bukharin came to defend Lenin's final writings as the assertion of a gradualist path to socialism. As Bukharin allegedly put it in conversation with Boris Nicolaevsky in 1936: 'The main point of his testament was that it is possible to arrive at Socialism without applying more force to the peasantry'.[18] Bukharin returned to the argument developed by Peter Struve at the end of the 1890s when he discussed the use of coercion after the socialist revolution, arguing that a socialist system of production could not be built on force as a permanent factor.

Khrushchev's Secret Speech on 25 February 1956 to the Twentieth Party Congress denounced Stalin's crimes, but failed to come to terms with the phenomenon of Stalinism itself. For a generation the speech came to represent the possibility that communism might be able to destalinize itself and take on a more honest and humanistic form. However, destalinization was halted, and partially reversed, by Leonid Brezhnev during his long rule (1964–82), and this evolutionary option remained closed until Mikhail Gorbachev from 1985 once again took up the issue of Stalin's crimes. By then destalinization was not enough, and the search for the truth about Soviet evolution veered towards the debunking of Lenin himself. The Chinese from 1978 were able to come to terms with Mao Zedong in a more subtle way, distinguishing between his 'great achievements' and his 'great errors', formulating with impressive mathematical accuracy that he was '70 per cent good and 30 per cent bad'. Thus Mao was both salvaged and condemned at the same time.

The Prague Spring of 1968 sought to create a 'socialism with a human face'. What this meant in practice was a radical redefinition of the leading role of the Party based on a more responsive relationship between the Party and society. The 'Action Programme' of the Czechoslovak Communist Party of 5 April criticized the practices of the communist regime, affirmed the principle of pluralism and respect for the views of the minority, accepted a broader scope for market relations, and above all insisted that the Party's right to rule came not from a one-off act of social seizure but by endless reciprocal relations with its constituents.[19] This idea of one-party pluralism was revived by Gorbachev twenty years later – twenty years too late, as soon became evident. For on 20–21 August 1968 the Soviet

Union and some of its Warsaw Pact allies invaded, and thus put an end to the most radical attempt to revive 'actually existing socialism'. This was one of the most fateful 'self-invasions' (or own goals) in history, suffocating the renewal of communism and condemning the USSR to a long stagnation that culminated in the dissolution of communist power itself.

The Prague Spring was followed by the 'normalization' of politics in Czechoslovakia and the proclamation of the Brezhnev Doctrine of limited sovereignty for communist countries. For the opposition the aim now was no longer to reform socialism but to transcend it. The end of reform socialism was marked in the period following the adoption of the Helsinki Final Act in August 1975. The Conference on Security and Cooperation in Europe (CSCE) had long been sought by the USSR to legitimate its post-war territorial gains and status, and this the Final Act did, but the price was the Soviet Union's acceptance of the 'third basket' human rights principles. Thus the Final Act represented the legal recognition of the post-war order symbolized by Yalta, but it set in place a dynamic that ultimately brought down that order: Helsinki first recognized Yalta, and then transcended it. Dissidents in Eastern Europe could now appeal to an international document ratified by their governments that enshrined a range of human and civil rights. This was the case with Charter 77 in Czechoslovakia, and with numerous other Helsinki monitoring groups throughout the region.

In the more open society that Poland became after 1956, a different and more sophisticated strategy was possible. For oppositionists like Adam Michnik spaces could be created in civil society where the logic of action did not so much directly challenge the party-state as ignore it, a policy of circumvention that proved extremely effective in delegitimating the communist regime and eroding its base in society.[20] The concept of civil society in the late communist period, however, had a dual charge: as a form of *resistance* and as a form of *emancipation*. In the latter sense the concept became a positive normative programme of social action (praxis) between communism and capitalism, a 'third way' that sought to recover politics for the social body itself. The idea of 'anti-politics' favouring workers' self-managagement and social self-administration was reminiscent, ironically, of Marx's own attempt to reappropriate alienated political power for society.[21] This was a genuinely 'self-limiting' understanding of a sphere of politics separate from the state, although it did not deny a legitimate role for the state and thus differed from Marx's view on its ultimate transcendence or the anarchist denial of a valid role for it whatsoever. While Havel's critique condemned modernity and technology in general, thinking on 'anti-politics' contained a specific critique of liberal capitalism as well as the general discontents of modern times, themes that have been taken up in an extensive Western literature on the subject.[22] The classic liberal distinction between state and society was maintained in specific repudiation of the spirit of 1917 and, indeed, 1789, where the revolution would 'devour its own children'.[23] As a form of resistance the recovery of the idea of civil society played a crucial part in the transcending revolution that led towards 1989–91, but as a form of emancipation the anti-political school of thought was itself transcended by the fall of communism. In the harsh light of postcommunism it was liberalism, with its necessary limitations on the scope of politics, that soon eclipsed hopes for a self-managing society.

In Western Europe, too, the communist movement was engaged in a process of transcending the limitations of its own ideology. Under Palmiro Togliatti the Italian Communist Party (PCI) was transformed into a mass party oriented towards government, a process accelerated by the adoption of Eurocommunism in the 1970s. The Rome declaration of the PCI and the French Communist Party (PCF) in November 1975 was the most unequivocal statement of the new approach, accepting above all the 'lay nature and democratic functioning of the State', together with party pluralism, democratic opposition and alternativity, and free and universal suffrage.[24] The old division between revolutionary and evolutionary socialism was transcended, although Eurocommunism remained loyal to a transformative vision as its ultimate aim. While Leninism represented the externalization of the revolution in an act of political violence, Eurocommunism, as it were, internalized revolution into the movement itself and thus ironically returned to a view that appears to be closer to Marx's own concept of revolution as transcendence and one that certainly drew on Gramsci's thinking. Under Enrico Berlinguer the PCI in the 1970s entered on the path of a 'historic compromise' and scored a notable success in the 1976 elections, yet was resolutely denied a share of power and thereafter its support declined. The transformation of the PCI accelerated under the leadership of Achille Occhetto from June 1988, bolstered now by the emergence of Gorbachev's *perestroika* (restructuring) in the USSR.

Gorbachev came to accept not only the basic themes of Euro-communism but also the fundamental principles of the Prague Spring's 'socialism with a human face'. *Glasnost* (openness) began with exposure of the Soviet past, starting with the Stalinist period and then moving on to criticize Lenin's rule as well, but later developed into a critique of the very basis of the regime. Alexander Tsipko, a former staff member of the Central Committee of the Communist Party, claimed that any Marxian socialism that sought to substitute central planning for the market was doomed to dictatorship. As far as he was concerned the warnings of Engels and Plekhanov about the failure that would follow a premature attempt to implement socialism were fully justified, but he took the argument further to suggest that any attempt to achieve revolutionary socialism would inevitably result in disaster.[25]

The philosophy of *perestroika* focused on the modernization of Soviet society and economy, with a new structure of management, a more responsive political system and some scope for cooperatives and joint enterprises. *Perestroika* represented the democratization of Soviet communism itself, to reforge the link broken by Lenin between socialism and democracy. An important aspect for Gorbachev was the moral renewal of socialism, although within certain limits. In his book, *Perestroika*, Gorbachev admitted that what he had inherited was not socialism but a centralized bureaucratic system that alienated the worker from production and politics.[26] He retrieved many of the principles that had informed the February 1917 revolution, including ultimately a broad commitment to democracy and inclusion. The trajectory of *perestroika* reversed that of 1917, with events moving rapidly from October to February, accompanied by the rehabilitation of the core Menshevik argument that it was impossible to skip stages in the transition from bourgeois democracy to socialism. The implication was that revolutionary socialism had failed, and that its whole developmental strategy had been based on the mistaken assumption that socialism could come *before* capitalism and act as its substitute. In numerous writings on the Third World, Soviet academics had already concluded that socialism should come after development, and thus the basic premiss of the October revolution was repudiated.[27] The whole Leninist revolutionary strategy was in effect repudiated, and 'revisionism', once so reviled, became the ruling ideology of reform. The problem came down to marketizing socialism, but even when the basic decision to move in this direction had been taken, no one knew how to achieve this monstrous hybrid, or even whether it was feasible.

While *perestroika* represented a profound reappraisal of the philosophical basis of the regime, it did not represent its deideologization: as Yegor Ligachev, one of Gorbachev's key subordinates before he became alarmed at the increasingly radical nature of *perestroika*, noted, 'Gorbachev often pointed out correctly that Soviet perestroika was a very important component of modern world history; it was created in the interests not only of the Soviet people but also for universal benefit'.[28] In fact, *perestroika* was the last great ideological campaign of the Soviet regime, drawing on the rich heritage of Marx's thinking and, indeed, commune democracy's emphasis on the soviets and popular self-management.[29] Gorbachev sought to recover the romantic mythology of revolution, insisting that *perestroika* was a 'revolution',[30] but with no detailed vision of the future or even of a better contemporary political practice, *perestroika* was by default permeated by a negative destructive logic. Gorbachev's concept of a 'revolution within the revolution' gutted the concept of revolution of all meaning. Not only was it a less than farcical replay of the earlier revolutionary tragedy, but the very logic of Leninist (and even Jacobin) revolution was inverted (see Chapter 6). Gorbachev's great achievement ultimately was to remove the limits on reform, and thus the system – even before it came crashing down in the wake of the failed coup of August 1991 – was well on the way to transcending itself.

Intimations of postcommunism were an essential part of communism itself, and in part explain the vigour with which the movement sought to suppress 'revisionist' thinking. From the very beginning 'renegades' were considered more dangerous enemies of the working class than acknowledged opponents on the other side of the barricades. The argument of this chapter has been that Marxism's own transcendence and fragmentation was linked with the failure of the communist project itself. The nature of that link, however, is a complex one. Clearly, the fall of the communist systems had something to do with the exhaustion of the theory of revolutionary socialism. But equally, the critiques discussed above represented attempts to revitalize the tradition of an alternative to capitalist democracy; yet they, too, failed permanently to regenerate the socialist project. The role of ideology in maintaining the

mature Soviet system or China since 1979 is in any case questionable. Without a revolutionary socialist ideology, however, these
were no longer communist systems in anything but name. There
were many roads to postcommunism, but the argument of this
chapter is that one of them (with numerous turnings and byways)
passed through communism itself.

3

The Communist
Experience

Transition theory focuses not only on outcomes but also on points of origin. In particular, the difference between post-totalitarian and other market-based post-authoritarian societies should be stressed. However decayed the 'totalitarian' societies may have become, they were marked to a greater or lesser extent by certain common features: no formal capitalist markets; no autonomous and legally guaranteed civil associations and processes of civil society (such as free trade unions or media); no autonomous structures in political society (such as political parties and legislatures); and everywhere the political fusion of communist parties with the state destroyed the principle of the separation of powers and endowed government with a destructively introspective dynamic that was ultimately to destroy them. In short, while these countries became recognizably modern (industrial, urban and literate), they lacked certain key features of modernity such as civic freedom, discursive rationality in policy-making, and private property and market rationality in the economy. It could well be concluded that Marxian Communism was little more than a dangerous irrelevance to the main problems facing modern society and susceptible to authoritarian forms of rule that inhibited all-round development of the societies and of the individuals who composed them. This was the conclusion, as we saw in the previous chapter, that a number of thinkers had reached even while communism as an idea and as a project was in full flood, and it was one that increasing numbers (including some of their leaders) increasingly shared.

The agony of communism

The trajectory of the Bolshevik revolution included numerous personal choices and surprises and confirmed Engels's observation that:

> People who boasted that they had *made* a revolution have always seen
> the next day that they had no idea what they were doing, that the
> revolution *made* did not in the least resemble the one they would have
> liked to have made.[1]

George Schöpflin's argument that the Soviet-type systems had vir-
tually nothing in common with socialism as defined in the West is
clearly misleading.[2] The Russian revolution was the first large-scale
attempt to implement Marxist revolutionary theory, the first to
build a society based on the rejection of Western modernity while
trying to fulfil it. This utopian project, as it is now called, displaced
political discourse from pragmatic reason towards a political practice that generated closure and exclusivity. Daniels details this
process in a chapter entitled 'The Long Agony of the Russian
Revolution',[3] Harding talks in terms of 'the Marxist-Leninist
Detour',[4] while Francis Fukuyama takes a characteristically robust
view: 'the total and manifest failure of communism forces us to ask
whether Marx's entire experiment was not a 150-year detour'.[5]

Any discussion of postcommunism must begin with some analysis of the practical experience of communism as the baseline against
which postcommunism develops. The concept of 'experience' is
today much trivialized, but we use it in this chapter to suggest the
experimental nature of communism and the interaction of ideals
and reality, aspiration and achievement, and the learning from the
past. Compared to the goals it set itself, the experience of communism was overwhelmingly negative. Communism failed to solve
the problem of economic development, unable in many cases even
to exploit catch-up factors while in relatively more advanced countries such as Czechoslovakia it imposed elements of demoderniza-
tion. It failed to close the gap between potential and actual
economic performance, and in some cases (Russia included) left
the countries relatively less developed in comparison with leading
rivals than they were before becoming communist. 'Actually existing socialism' became a pale imitation of the consumer societies
found in the West – and why endure the imitation when the real
thing is possible? The communist pattern of development can be
dubbed 'mismodernization' – this is not to suggest that there is only

one correct path but to stress that fundamental features of effective modernization were missing: the bias against innovation; the emphasis on quantitative growth; low productivity of labour; enormous waste and poor quality; lack of coordination; and where 'planning', according to Blackburn, 'simply imposed a thoughless incrementalism, with each plant or enterprise seeking to increase its output of goods or services compared with the previous period'.[6] This was in effect modernization without modernity, lacking some key ingredients of complex modernization.

As for the political level, the communist experiment here failed every basic test of statecraft and effectiveness, ultimately failing the sternest test of all – the ability to survive. It failed to solve the problems of political democracy, effective participation and inclusion, and in the case of Czechoslovakia, the Soviet Union and Yugoslavia, it failed to sustain viable federal states that could withstand the dissolution of the communist regimes. The failure was also one of imagination – in Sassoon's words: 'Not one novelty worth writing or thinking about had been envisioned or predicted by the European socialist movement'.[7] Above all, communism failed to resolve the core problem that it set itself, namely the overcoming of alienation and the achievement of freedom. Communism was indeed in *agonia*, mental anguish at the gulf between its ideals, the reality it found itself in and the reality that it became.

Theoretical Communism also failed to sustain a positive emancipatory programme of social change. While few would deny the pungency and in many respects the accuracy (accompanied by some drastic inadequacies) of Marx's critique of capitalism, its imputed model of a better society was riddled with problems. To take just one important example: how would a society that had abolished the private ownership of the means of production and the market manage the common economic affairs of that society? This was the question tackled by Alec Nove, and his answer was that each possible solution entailed so many deleterious consequences as to constitute a worse hazard than the problem they sought to overcome.[8] Marxian Communism had been devised in the pre-corporate age of entrepreneurial capitalism, and had little to say about the management of complex economic systems in mass democratic societies.

The vision of a self-managing society, outlined in Marx's *Civil War in France* and taken up by Lenin in *The State and Revolution* of August–September 1917, where he argued that every cook could manage the affairs of the post-revolutionary society, reflected an astonishing naivety in regard to the advancing bureaucratization of modern governance. As calls for political emancipation they endure as powerful reminders of the lure of a transparent, egalitarian and participatory society, but the strangely archaic prescriptions are an equally powerful reminder of how the ideal of Marxist-Leninist commune democracy refused to engage with the science of politics itself – of mediating between conflicting interests, of separating powers, of establishing checking mechanisms on the exercise of power, of defending the inviolability of the individual and the like. These essentially liberal concerns were by no means rejected by Marx (indeed, his main charge against liberalism was that it was unable to fulfil its own promises in capitalist society), but failed to find any serious echo in his political philosophy.

Any analysis of the communist experience must be sensitive to the enormous variety of 'actually existing socialisms' – from the stifling gerontocracy of Brezhnev's last years to Cuba's personalized but relatively benevolent authoritarianism and the murderous 'excesses' of Mao Zedong's Cultural Revolution in China. It must also take into account the evolution of policy, including the complex interaction of ideology, pragmatism and national interests. Lenin's own thinking, for example, was in a constant process of evolution, always responsive to changing circumstances and ready to defy his own party to achieve what he perceived to be the best interests of the revolution.

Above all, we are faced with the problem of Stalinism. It is too glib to dissociate Marx from any responsibility for the evolution of practical communism into its Stalinist variant – after all, as many Russian reformers argued during *perestroika*, Stalinism did not emerge out of Buddhism! It had its roots firmly in Marx's tendency to collapse complex patterns of historical evolution and political differentiation into simplistic economic categories. In particular, the sphere of individual autonomy and civil association denoted by the concept of civil society in Marx's thinking was reduced to no more than the exploitative relations of the capitalist mode of production. The economism deeply rooted in Marx's thinking flourished under Stalin, when socialism was defined less as the quality of relations between *people* (the humanistic variant espoused later by Dubček and Gorbachev) than between *things* – primarily the common ownership of the means of production. However, while there is undoubtedly a line from Marx running through Lenin and on to Stalin, this is not the only possible path of evolution. Trotskyists, for example, insist that Stalinism represented the adaptation of the doctrine to Russia's backward economy and political culture – 'Marxism reflected in a samovar', as Trotsky put it. Backwardness meant that the original emancipatory agenda had to be subordinated to developmental purposes, while the legacy of Tsarism allowed a corrupt and self-seeking bureaucratic class to emerge that saw Stalin as the embodiment of their aspirations – or so Trotsky argued in *The Revolution Betrayed* in 1936. Thus Trotsky was able to separate Stalin from Lenin and other socialist precursors. Yet the analysis is profoundly flawed, leaving out of account 'Stalinist' tendencies under Lenin (the establishment of the secret police and prison camps, mass shootings, bureaucratization and so on) and denying Stalin any political autonomy, or indeed any great abilities at all. Stalin was far from being the creature of any bureaucratic class and instead was a creative and highly intelligent (although unspeakably cruel) political leader. As E.H. Carr argued, without Stalin the October revolution would have run into the sands of peasant Russia. Most great revolutionary leaders have to betray elements of the revolution to save its substantive gains.

In China a rather different model emerged. According to Jack Gray:

> The first book on Marxism read by the young Mao was Thomas Kirkup's *History of Socialism*, in which he argued that socialist visions of the future involved an unresolved contradiction between the idea of Saint-Simonian technocratic élitism and the communitarian concept of Robert Owen. Kirkup chose the latter, and so did Mao.[9]

In *The Ten Great Relationships*, written in 1956, Mao denounced the idea of giving priority to heavy industry – 'If you are really serious about heavy industry, you will give priority to agriculture and light industry' – and he followed this up with a trenchant critique of Stalinism out of which emerged the Great Leap Forward (1958–61) and its associated famine in which an estimated 50 million perished. Maoism represented the adaptation of Marxism to Chinese conditions, but the adaptation of the ideology and the formal structures of the regimes to specific social and political realities was a process that took place everywhere. Already Merle Fainsod's work on the Smolensk archive revealed a complex pattern of local interests in

the 1930s, the weakness of rural Party organization and many
expressions of popular discontent with the regime, prompting him
to revise his view of the Stalinist regime as totalitarian towards
something he variously termed 'inefficient totalitarianism' or a
'totalitarian façade'.[10] Generalizing on her work on Romania, the
anthropologist Katherine Verdery examined the way informal
social structures evolved to allow the formal system to work. Well
before 1989 there had been a seepage of power from the ministries
to the enterprises and associated informal networks, and for the
managers the dissolution of communist power allowed them to
become owners – one of the key factors in Verdery's view that
explains the rapid collapse. It also explains the shift under postcommunism from socialism to what she calls feudalism, as these
functional social groups legalized their power.[11]

The fall – the transcending revolutions of 1989–91

The precise exit path from communism differed between countries,
yet certain broad commonalities can be observed. In Eastern
Europe communism's failure was due both to domestic and
external factors. With the exception of Albania and Yugoslavia, the
post-war communist systems were established primarily under the
auspices of the Soviet Army. In most cases the domestic roots of the
communist parties were weak and the regimes were perceived as
alien and lacking national legitimacy. While democracy was at the
heart of the 1989 revolutions, so too was patriotism, the attempt to
regain national autonomy and to restore the state's place as a fully-
fledged actor in the international system. Although the most successful and most durable form of communism was the indigenous
national communism of Russia, Yugoslavia, China, North Korea,
Vietnam and Cuba, the case of Yugoslavia demonstrates that the
failure of communism lies not only in its imposed character, or even
in its inability to respond to domestic circumstances and local conditions. Communism in Yugoslavia had evolved considerably, and
for a time appeared to offer a viable 'third way' between capitalism
and Soviet-style state socialism.

The failure of the communist systems lies primarily not in their
lack of national legitimacy, but in the broader lack of political,
social and economic viability. Communism appeared unable to
resolve the most pressing questions of political inclusion, social

justice and advanced economic modernization. By 1989, quite simply, the great majority of the populations, and not a few communists themselves, were no longer interested in the regimes' continuance. Socialist rhetoric notwithstanding, the societies were marked by growing inequalities, the emergence of privileged and increasingly closed self-perpetuating élites, and declining economic performance. Communist systems had laid the foundations of modernization, although in a centralized, bureaucratized and distorted way, but the emphasis on heavy industry and the absence of regional specialization ultimately meant that the systems could no longer fulfil the promise of improved standards of living and, with the option of mass terror no longer realistic, made their exits from the stage of history.

Ekiert observes that, in the 1980s,

> the Polish state experienced a fate similar to those of all military dictatorships. It defined itself as a classical 'regime exceptional' [sic], and by doing this it abandoned communist regimes' 'historical mission' to offer a permanent alternative to political democracy and market economy. Its only justification was based on the claim to deliver efficiency, a better economic performance, and therefore better standards of living and economic security, as well as to put an end to injustice, corruption, and anarchy. When this claim failed, there was nothing left to justify the necessity and indispensability of the oppressive political rule.[12]

A similar argument is proposed by Leslie Holmes, who notes that late communist systems had mostly lost their grand future-oriented beliefs and instead promised improved standards of living and welfarism, an approach that he labels 'eudaemonic', the attempt 'by political leaders to legitimate their rule in terms of the political order's performance'.[13] Polish communism had suffered an almost permanent crisis of legitimacy, but the problem that took an extreme form there was evident elsewhere.

In the USSR there was decay from within and the regime became one of crisis management. Communist regimes were systems of power and not of order, with order here defined, following Eckstein, as congruence between the authority patterns of government and other units of society.[14] We need to go further, however, since the problem was not so much the lack of congruence between the two types of authority patterns as a growing divergence between the definition of the legitimate scope and purpose of governing power and the views of a growing body of opinion in society. While the Soviet system may well have been a utopia in power, ultimately it found itself trying to impose order from outside and failed to find adequate political institutions of utopia. Marxism's lack of a developed theory of politics provoked the state failure of Soviet-type systems. There was no shortage of state bodies, but what they lacked was an organic and responsive relationship with society and each other.[15] By the end communist systems were typified by old men clinging to power. Communism, as Stephen Hanson has suggested, was a struggle against time,[16] but ultimately it was defeated by entropy as regimes that considered themselves masters of time gave up the unequal struggle.

This is not the place to go into detail on the mechanics of the fall of the European communist systems in 1989–91, but several points may be noted. There has been a long, if unilluminating, discussion over the nature of the 'revolutions' of these years. Timothy Garton Ash coined the term 'refolution' to indicate the combination of reformist political style and the profoundly revolutionary consequences of the events.[17] Jürgen Habermas dubbed the process 'the rectifying revolution', an attempt to overcome the distortions of 'actually existing socialism' while recognizing that the logic of capitalist accumulation battered down the 'Chinese walls' (as the *Communist Manifesto* described the way cheap commodities forced all nations to adopt the capitalist mode of production) of the post-capitalist societies as much as it did of the pre-capitalist ones.[18] Holmes characterized them as 'rejective' revolutions, which in the case of Eastern Europe becomes doubly rejective, repudiating not only communism itself but also the Soviet domination with which it was associated. Our argument goes beyond these formulations. Following the logic of our previous chapter, where we discussed 'the long transcendence', there was a profound logic not only in the mere fact of the fall of the communist regimes, but also in the manner in which they were disposed of. These were transcending revolutions, not only overcoming the communist systems of power themselves but also repudiating the political practices and logic on which they were based.

The transcending revolutions were rich in political practices that gave rise to what we shall call the 'anti-revolutions' of this period (see Chapter 6). One of these was the repudiation of violence and the practice of the peaceful mass demonstration. Significant violence was witnessed only in Romania, where the revolution against Nicolae Ceauşescu was perhaps less transcending than an old-fashioned revolt against tyranny. Elsewhere, the revolutions were directed at the more subtle and systemic features of communist despotism. A second feature was the prevalence of 'forum politics', beginning with the various 'round tables' that negotiated their way out of communism and culminating in the formation of 'anti-political' bodies such as Civic Forum in the Czech lands and Citizens against Violence in Slovakia in November 1989. The third point follows from this, namely the negotiated nature of the exit from communism in a number of countries, in particular Poland and Hungary. Nowhere in Eastern Europe were there organized counter-élites or serious attempts to sustain a counter-ideology: *nomenklatura* élites had ceased to believe in the viability of the old ways and had already achieved a mental liberation from revolutionary socialism, an inner transcendence that pre-empted a Tiananmen Square solution. Although, fourthly, the regimes were permeated by corruption it was not this as such that brought them down;[19] there are plenty of deeply corrupt regimes that appear to prosper. Undoubtedly, as von Beyme notes, the market logic of corruption in a planned economy comes into contradiction with the *nomenklatura* élite.[20] More importantly, corruption and its associated clientilistic relations represented a *social* adaptation of the regime to society and it was this that subverted any residual claims of the *political* system to a vanguardist role. These were, fifthly, popular revolutions as well, witnessed perhaps most vividly in the candle-lit marches in Leipzig and culminating in the way the Berlin Wall was in effect willed out of existence on 9 November 1989. What had technically been only a relaxation of travel restrictions was converted by the people into the transcendence of the Wall itself – and with it of communism.

The dissolution of the Soviet regime had characteristics of its own derived from its autonomous character. While pressure from below for change was far from negligible and its economic problems were similar, its multinational character and its role in the world clearly imbued the fall here with a distinctive dynamic. It might well be argued (and each policy area finds its advocates) that the economic system retained some mileage, that an earlier and more radical approach might have resolved the knot of ethno-federal relations, and so on. The larger failure was at the level of decisions and the state (the polity), which simply could not adapt to its national community (as the regime could in China or Vietnam) because of fundamental disagreements about what constituted that national community. The exit from communism in Eastern Europe was a transcending revolution, but in the USSR (and some Asian countries) where communism had deep indigenous roots it became something stronger: a self-transcending revolution. In the USSR a section of the old élite not only lost its allegiance to the old system but embarked on its self-emancipation, thereby converting privileges into property and power into formally more pluralistic forms of political interaction. The propertization of old élites took place throughout Eastern Europe,[21] but here the conversion of the *nomenklatura* into a new type of dominant class has been seen as the defining feature of the changes.[22] From this perspective, the Soviet case represents a semi-evolutionary exit from communism, where the formal structures of the old political system disappeared in their entirety but the old élites adapted to the new system and imbued it with many of the attitudes of the past. More profoundly, in a civilizational sense much of society was prepared for the change and thus rendered it smoother if no less traumatic.

The transcendence of communism almost everywhere took unrevolutionary forms, although the consequences were profoundly revolutionary. We shall explore this paradox later, but for now stress that the transfer of power was achieved with a minimal amount of bloodshed and above all without any sustained repression against the outgoing élite and its repressive apparatus (except, partially, in East Germany). A classic revolutionary insurgency proved unnecessary for the simple reason (except, again partially, in Romania) that there were few willing to risk their lives defending the old regime. The central factor here is that the old élites in effect transformed themselves into the new through what we have dubbed systemic self-transcendence from within. It is for this reason that, however much institutional restructuring might have taken place in postcommunist countries, their aura and feel remain remarkably similar to those of the old system. In appearance at least, these were very much 'incomplete' revolutions. The common complaint under postcommunism is that everything has changed and nothing has changed, and, in the sense suggested above, both statements are true.

Self-transcendence and beyond

China is one of five recognizably Marxist-Leninist states – the others being North Korea, Vietnam, Laos and Cuba – engaged in the monumental project of the self-transcendence of communism. We use the term 'self-transcendence' advisedly, because the mainly Western European process of transcendence described in Chapter 2 had little impact in China. Self-transcendence is generated by indigenous concerns and imperatives, and thus postcommunism here takes a very different form than in the European communist states. The distinctive aetiology of Chinese postcommunism reflects the characteristics of Chinese communism itself. China is a communist state introducing capitalism: one of the most eloquent paradoxes of our 'postcommunist' times and an ironic comment on the fate of revolutionary socialism itself.

The self-transcending revolutions of Asia are being achieved not by the dissolution of the regimes and the conversion of their powers into new forms, but by the communist systems themselves leading the gradual adaptation to market-oriented national development tasks. Chinese communism had always been torn between an unabashedly developmentalist strategy (the Deng Xiaoping line) and Mao's permanent class struggle line that subordinated developmental tasks to broader problems of communist construction. Deng's triumph over his rivals from 1978 and the launching of the 'four modernizations' in 1979, although retaining the leading role of the Party and a commitment to socialism, already a decade before the fall of communism in Eastern Europe outlined a distinctive route towards the future. The crushing of the democracy movement in Tiananmen Square in June 1989 confirmed that Chinese history marched to a rhythm of its own. China is the clearest example of the possibility of a wholly evolutionary exit from communism.

In Vietnam a process of economic reforms (termed *doi moi*, meaning 'renovation') from 1986 converted what had been an inflation-ridden economy of shortages into one of the Asian 'tigers', with economic growth averaging 8 per cent per annum, with strong capital inflows, and finally at peace with its neighbours. Corruption, however, became endemic and calls for political reform were condemned by the communist leadership as 'peaceful evolution' by hostile forces allegedly intent on undermining its control.

Cambodian communism had emerged out of the fearsome forces unleashed by the long war in neighbouring Vietnam and, although recognizably in the communist tradition, took such an extreme form because of its peculiar genealogy that it deserves special study. Much the same can be said of North Korean communism. Both were bound up with native peasant traditions, the distorted and crude appreciation of a foreign ideology by deracinated intellectuals, the play of great power and regional rivalries, the legacy of colonialism, and exaggerated leaderism that in the North Korean case reached bizarre heights. The strange metamorphosis of the concept of the party's leading role into the extraordinarily primitive but equally extreme application of a few ideas of the revolutionary socialist canon into dogmas of such rigidity makes even Stalin appear a flexible opportunist in comparison. The death of Pol Pot in April 1998 put an end to the Khmer Rouge as a serious force in Cambodian politics, while Kim Il Sung's death in 1994 led to a protracted end-game in North Korea in which his son, Kim Jong Il presided over famine and economic collapse.

With the voluntary abdication of power through elections by the Sandinista government in Nicaragua, in the Americas only Cuba remained committed to a non-capitalist path, although even here the market was surreptitiously reintroduced in key foreign currency earning sectors such as tourism. Fidel Castro's regime, since coming to power in 1959, had always been a mix of nationalism, socialism and old-fashioned caudillo-style leadership politics. The regime, however, provided standards of health, education, welfare services, public transport and egalitarianism that were unique in the hemisphere – but the only problem was that the economy simply could not sustain them. The loss of Soviet subsidies after 1991 forced a drastic readjustment, particularly as American sanctions remained in force. The problem of 'human rights', moreover, was not simply a weapon with which Cuban émigrés in Florida could beat Castro's regime but represented a challenge to democratize socialism on the island. Political prisoners remained incarcerated, freedom of speech remained limited and the Committees for the Defence of the Revolution still made life miserable for many. Already symptoms that prefigured the fall of the communist regimes in Eastern Europe are prevalent in Cuba, including an aged leadership sure of its own infallibility (something much in evidence at the Cuban Communist Party's Fifth Congress in October 1997). Only the fusion of the socialist achievements of the past and the democracy of the future could enable something to be salvaged from the Cuban experiment with socialism – but this would in all probability be a step too far for Castro and other self-appointed guardians of 'socialism'.

In Africa adulterated forms of Soviet-style socialism had been established in Angola, Mozambique, Madagascar, Congo-Brazzaville, Benin and Ethiopia, where regimes adopted Marxism-Leninism as the ruling ideology and declared themselves to be building socialism. Nine other countries declared themselves socialist: Algeria, Libya, Cape Verde, Guinea-Bissau, Guinea, São Tomé and Principe, Zambia, Tanzania and Seychelles. The experiment with 'African socialism' had begun with Ghana under Kwame Nkrumah in the 1950s and continued with Julius Nyerere's impressive experiment in self-reliance in Tanzania following independence in 1961. In Guinea Sékou Touré had established one of Africa's most oppressive regimes, banning all private trade and conducting all business through cooperatives supervised by the state, until in 1977 a revolt forced the abandonment of 'socialist' development. Elections in 1992 saw the old regime ousted in Congo-Brazzaville, but elsewhere more violent overthrows took place. With the exception of war-torn Angola, all these regimes fell or were modified in the 1990s, and what came to be seen as the false path of applying an ideology of developed societies to African conditions was everywhere abandoned. Although Tanzania became one of the most egalitarian societies in Africa, the economy was stifled by a ubiquitous state bureaucracy and after Nyerere's long rule was at the same level of development as when he gained power. In Ethiopia the rule of the self-proclaimed communists was accompanied by the usual mass murder and terror, until the regime was finally overthrown in 1991 by a revolt of the regions. The experience of revolutionary socialism in Africa was no less disappointing than in Europe. It played little part in the decolonization struggle, and thereafter did not unlock the doors to development. Its strident anti-Westernism and insistence on 'native' paths transformed African communism into the ideology of archaic tyranny.

'Actually existing socialism' was characterized by two key features: its machinery of terror that had active or quiescent phases but which was never abolished, and its economic inefficiency. The relationship between political organization and the powerful social

dynamics of modernizing societies was left vague in Marx's thinking, and in the systems that ruled in his name later, the gulf between
the teleological purpose of the governing power and the subtle
relationships that characterize the relationship between state and
society in coherent systems was lacking. Communist regimes found
themselves in what turned out to be an irresolvable bind: as long as
they were committed to achieving some transcendent purpose ('the
building of communism') they found themselves in an adversarial
relationship with important sectors of society; but if the regime
adapted to the aspirations of society (it is immaterial what precisely
these were, although by the end, under the influence of the success
of the post-war West, the striving for democracy was not the least
significant), then its very existence was redundant. Who needs a
monopolistic power system seeking to achieve some other-wordly
goal with indifferent economic results when more efficient and less
painful alternatives were everywhere on view? The problem could
have been finessed by the development of a democratic socialist
combination of Western rationality and Soviet socialism, but by the
time Gorbachev gave the green light for experiments in this direction it proved, for reasons whose details remain disputed, too late.
The communist experience, both as a subjective appreciation of the
attempt to implement a form of Marxian socialism and as a social
experiment on the grandest of all possible scales, proved a tortured
failure and was unable to sustain its claims to provide a viable
alternative to Western capitalist modernity. It is to the consequences of that failure and the attempts to overcome them that we
now turn.

Postcommunism in Practice

If Kautsky in 1902 had been concerned with how the common affairs of the socialist state would be managed the day after the *revolution*, our concern here is the problems facing the societies the day after the *anti-revolution*. If the move towards communism, launched in Russia in 1917, in Eastern Europe between 1944 and 1948, in China in 1949 and in Cuba in 1959, can be dubbed *permanent transition*, advancing towards an endlessly receding horizon, the postcommunist change can be characterized as *total transition*, simultaneously affecting politics, the economy, society and the international orientations of the states concerned. While the practice of liberal democracy may well be open to endless improvement, the actual transition in the case of the move towards capitalist democracy is not permanent in the narrow sense that an end point is relatively easy to identify. Unlike most post-colonial societies, the majority of postcommunist states appeared to enjoy greater advantages, above all in the field of 'human capital', with educated and technologically sophisticated populations and experienced ruling élites. These advantages in practice proved difficult to realize, and the embarkation point of postcommunism on the journey to modern capitalist democracy appeared as unenviable as that of post-colonialism, especially since the very statehood of the majority of post-Soviet and Balkan countries was in question. The starting point of postcommunism was a litany of absences:

> What was missing, in particular, was private property, a bourgeoisie, organized interest groups, political parties, unions (aside from rump unions), and informal associations and organizations. Also missing was rule of law and a rational and politically accountable bureaucracy.[1]

Jowitt adds his voice to the gloomy prognosis, arguing that the
Leninist legacy '*and* the initial charismatic ethical opposition to it
favor an authoritarian, not a liberal democratic way of life'.[2] China
followed the example set by Bismarck's Germany of creating a
market economy before democratization, whereas Eurasian postcommunism is tormented by the *simultaneity* problem.

The postcommunist syndrome – postcommunism versus democratization

The focus in this chapter is on practical postcommunism, the challenges facing countries that have either left communism or are in
the process of doing so.[3] While there is what might be called a
generic postcommunist syndrome, marked by the collapse of
future-oriented emancipatory ideologies and pusillanimity in the
face of the global reach of capitalism, there are also postcommunist
experiences specific to each country. In some areas, notably parts of
the Balkans and in Central Asia, countries appear to have entered
not postcommunism at all but precommunism, while elsewhere in
Asia the exit from communism is being negotiated in a distinctive
way that forces us to refine our model of postcommunism.

Are we witnessing a transition to democracy in the postcommunist countries comparable to transitions elsewhere, above all in
the other 'third wave' transitions of Southern Europe and Latin
America?[4] There are as many differences between the individual
countries of these regions as there are between postcommunist
countries. In their recent transitological study covering all three
areas, moreover, Linz and Stepan stress the triadic relationship
between the simultaneous development of statehood, nationalism
and democracy in the postcommunist states.[5] Valerie Bunce has firm
views on the issue: 'The key question, then, is whether the differences constitute variations on a common process – that is, transitions
from dictatorship to democracy – or altogether different processes
– that is, democratization versus what could be termed postcommunism'.[6] Are the differences merely ones of degree or in kind? The
fact that postcommunist societies faced total transitions might
suggest that the latter view is more appropriate, but when examined
through the prism of universal postcommunism there is a commonality of problems that transcends the issue of whether a specific

country was communist or not. There are common challenges facing all countries irrespective of the past.

For area studies specialists there are specific problems facing former communist countries derived equally from their former communism and the historical traditions of the countries themselves. The different 'modes of extrication'[7] from communism were determined by past crises and their legacies. We need to speak the language and understand the cultures and histories, and only then can we approach an understanding of specific patterns of political development. Perhaps the greatest difference between the postcommunist transitions and those elsewhere concerns the roles played by the military and the existing capitalist class. In addition to the 'triple transition' identified by Claus Offe (changes in regime, economy and, in some cases, borders as well),[8] the whole sociopolitical terrain of postcommunist countries is subject to change as 'bureaucratic crypto-politics'[9] gives way to more pluralistic forms of interaction. The whole gamut of civil associations has had to be reconstituted from scratch. While there were few defenders of the old regime in Central Europe, where the main conflicts were between 'proto-democratic' actors,[10] this was not the case elsewhere. In Russia and Ukraine the strength of the communist parties testified perhaps not so much to support for the old regime as to the security communism had provided in its last years for the majority.

In the European postcommunist countries the issue of sequencing was not really an option, and the simultaneous attempt to introduce democracy and a market economy was forced upon them. In Asia, however, the issue of what political regime is most effective at managing economic reform was answered in a distinctive way. The impressive growth rates registered in China and Vietnam (together with Taiwan, Singapore and some other countries until the late 1990s) suggested that quasi-authoritarian governments may be better equipped to manage the transformative process. However, the pattern of capitalism first, democracy second itself generates tensions that lack a political mode of resolution. Everywhere the multiplicity of changes move at different speeds, promoting distortions and political instability. Ralf Dahrendorf has analysed these problems in terms of the 'dilemma of the three clocks'. In 'the hour of the lawyer' the constitutional and political framework is established during the course of several months; in 'the hour of the economist' the rudiments of a market economy are built in a process that may take five or six years; and finally, in 'the hour of the citizen' the social impulses of civil society are regenerated in the course of a process that will inevitably take decades.[11] Hopes that the fall of communism would mean that 'history had at last come to its senses' gave way to anxiety about the consequences of the fall, and it is these that we now examine.

Economic transformation

Economic liberalization has been the keynote of our age. Franco's economic liberalization programme of 1957 can be considered a harbinger of postcommunist transitions and an early case of 'shock therapy'. Predominant was the 'Washington consensus', the term coined by John Williamson to describe the neo-liberal policies adopted by a number of Latin American states in the mid-1980s focusing on fiscal and monetary discipline, currency convertibility, price and trade liberalization and the privatization of state enterprises.[12] These policies have been adopted to varying degrees by India and other countries that had pursued socialist-inclined developmental strategies. Economies were opened to international influences and domestic monopolies broken up and privatized. In the postcommunist countries this was accompanied by great falls in economic activity, with Russian gross national product halving by 1995 and then hovering between recession and growth until plunged into renewed crisis in August 1998, while some were able to register strong growth later. The problem is to identify what part of the decline was caused by the traumas of transition and what came from systemic long-term factors. Poland had long been faced with economic slowdown (with a 25 per cent fall in national income in 1978–82), which, combined with the recession of 1989–91, reduced per capita national product to the level of 1973. Even before the fall of communism most economies were suffering from what Kazimierz Poznanski identifed as structural 'growth fatigue' provoked not only by the temporal decline in the state-planned systems' ability to mobilize investment resources for growth when faced by pressures for higher wages and greater consumption spending, but also by the increasing incoherence of the institutions of the party-state.[13] An 'idle cycle' (Poznanski) of economic reforms in countries such as Poland and Russia only exacerbated the fundamental problems facing the planned economies of the region.

The onset of postcommunism was everywhere accompanied by the dismantling of the state planning machinery, while there was inevitably a lag before the full panoply of market-based mechanisms could be established. It was in this chaotic initial period that some countries launched what are conventionally described as 'shock therapy' policies, the rapid liberalization of prices and the reduction of subsidies accompanied by attempts to achieve a tight fiscal policy to rein in inflation and to achieve macroeconomic stabilization. Deflationary policies intensified what had already been profound economic crises. The early period was dominated by debates over whether liberalization should precede or follow privatization and demonopolization (the latter position being advocated by Grigorii Yavlinskii in Russia), yet most countries, including Russia and Poland, did not have the luxury of being in a position to choose. To paraphrase the Churchill hypothesis on democracy, shock therapy was the worst policy except for all the others. This certainly was the view of one of the most influential of the postcommunist economists, Jeffrey Sachs, who in numerous publications defended the 'Washington consensus' package of economic reforms, insisting that only a rapid and comprehensive transition would be able to overcome the distortions of command economies. A specialist on Third World debt, from July 1985 he had advised the Bolivian government on a proto-postcommunist programme of shock therapy. In Poland from June 1989, he advised the Solidarity leadership on how to overcome the crisis.

The issue of sequencing has been the subject of bitter debates. Leszek Balcerowicz, the architect of Polish shock therapy of 1989–91, defended his view that a complete and rapid systemic transformation was the only possible reform strategy in the exit from communism.[14] Political factors were central to this approach, based on the need to achieve market-oriented reforms during the initial period of high political mobilization following the fall of communism. Others have insisted that shock therapy entailed massive and unforeseen consequences, including deindustrialization and high unemployment (although the latter was often hidden). The political consequences have also been noted, since rapid transformation has usually been accompanied by authoritarian policies. Gradualists insist that a more democratic and inclusive transitional programme would allow the reforms to take root and would limit the opportunies for rent-seeking and corruption.

The defenders of the rapid path note that shock therapy in most cases is a misnomer anyway, since political pressures usually forced modifications, and point to the obvious failures of countries that have lagged behind in imposing essential liberalizing economic reforms. Ukraine appears a classic case where political pressures have undermined the logic of marketization, trapping the country into an extended period of 'neither plan nor market'. Belarus's unreformed economy under Alyaksandr Lukashenka only survived due to Russian subsidies, inflationary monetary emission and creative accounting.

Economic transformation included a number of features that have been pursued with varying commitment by most postcommunist countries. The liberalization of prices and economic activity, often accompanied by attempts to reduce the dominance of the communist era monopolies, is at the heart of postcommunist transformation. Liberalization, especially in its early stages, encouraged the massive growth of rent seeking – that is, the exploitation of distortions in the economy. In a number of countries, including Russia, rent-seeking élites in effect became the new ruling class. In China, with a dual economy, rent-seeking luxuriated in the interface between the controlled state sector and the liberalized parts of the economy.

The liberalization of foreign trade is usually seen as a way of introducing the standards and institutions of the world market into the transition economy. Trade liberalization is seen as both a means – the introduction of competition and 'capitalist efficiency – into the domestic market, and an end – making available a standard of material goods hitherto inaccessible to the citizen of communist societies.[15] The experience of the 'rapid liberalizers' – Poland, Czechoslovakia, Hungary and Vietnam – suggests that there is much to support this argument, although the persistence of trade deficits should be noted. Elsewhere, for example in Russia, the opening up of the domestic market has tended to squeeze out domestic products and, although tariff barriers have been used, not enough time has been allowed for domestic producers to modernize to meet the challenge of imports. The postcommunist era has coincided with the establishment of the vigorously anti-protectionist regime of the World Trade Organization which limits a country's ability to defend domestic producers. Selective association agreements with the European Union (EU), together with the latter's aggressive anti-dumping policies, have reinforced the pressure for open economies. This has not allowed the comparative advantages of a given economy to become consolidated, and left them prey to the more mature capitalist economies.

Fiscal stabilization, including the attempt to maintain the value of the domestic currency and to achieve foreign convertibility, has been hampered by the difficulty of creating, usually *ex nihilo*, tax systems. The inability of the Russian state, for example, to collect taxes, accompanied by a confiscatory tax structure, had by the end of the 1990s become the single greatest problem of the economy. With federal revenues falling to only 11 per cent of gross domestic product by early 1998 and federal government expenditure falling to only 14.5 per cent, the state found it increasingly difficult to carry out its basic responsibilities.

Communism had been obsessed by the question of property rights, what Zbigniew Brzezinski dubs the 'grand oversimplification' that located the origin of all evil in private property.[16] Ironically, this was a concern now adopted by the postcommunist regimes and their Western advisers who considered state property the greatest obstacle to market rationality. The privatization of state-owned enterprises was the most complex task, accompanied usually by insider dealings and corruption. A number of different official privatization schemes were tried but the most prevalent was the one that bore no official name – the 'stealing' or 'grabbing' of state assets by former enterprise directors and others with the leverage to convert public assets into private ones. Privatization at root, it must be stressed, was as much a political as an economic act, intended to break the old economic structures and, in the words of one study of the subject, 'to establish the individual economic freedom that underlies political freedom and helps keep the power of the state in check'.[17]

Once large-scale privatization was over, the emphasis shifted to issues of corporate governance and shareholder control. Privatization was intended to ensure clear property rights for capitalist managers who could then restructure an enterprise along commercial lines, but only in a few cases did it meet this aim, and certainly not in Russia. The point was to promote the microeconomic adjustment of firms and to encourage investment responsive to the demands of the market. Enterprise restructuring was often delayed to avoid unemployment.

For some Eastern European countries there was the problem of restitution to previous owners of property illegally confiscated by the communist regimes. Conflicts over ownership in some countries delayed repairs and investment.

Social policies have been developed, including welfare, unemployment and pensions, that approximate those found in more mature capitalist societies, although tailored to the resources and capacity of each individual state. Under state socialism the enterprise had been responsible for a range of social facilities, including public housing and kindergartens, that they now tried to transfer to the local authorities.

Much of the future depended on the creation of new businesses, and the encouragement of entrepreneurialism was something all postcommunist countries came to sooner or later. In Poland and China small businesses were the motor of economic development.

While the new business sector was of crucial importance, the legacy of state socialism endowed most postcommunist economies with large industrial sectors. Irrespective of the political changes, the challenge of moving from a smokestack to a service economy would have faced these societies. By the mid-1990s services already constituted 70 per cent of American and 60 per cent of British gross domestic product. However, deindustrialization can hardly be a desired outcome of the transition. In China the gulf between the state sector, with 305,000 enterprises of which 118,000 were industrial, and the dynamic private sector not only was one of the forms of property ownership but also reflected, like geological layers, the economic history of the country.

The economic crisis did, however, have one unintended advantage, namely a reduction in pollution, in particular in the lignite-burning areas of Bohemia and East Germany. This was likely to be only a temporary phenomenon since the societies appeared committed to achieving Western standards of consumption and economic activity with little regard to the abusive environmental consequences of the pursuit of unrestrained economic growth. The wasteful pattern of Soviet-style economic development allowed huge areas to remain as semi-wilderness, with one-third of the landscape in Central and Eastern Europe still relatively undeveloped natural lands, but capitalism, with its obsession with the efficient exploitation of resources, would be hardly likely to leave them undisturbed. In conditions of weak state capacity in the transitional period, moreover, existing environmental legislation was often not enforced.

By no means the least important factor was the adjustment of the state's own role in the economy, including its relationship with the central bank, as part of the establishment of a new balance between the *dirigisme* of the past and the neo-liberal minimalism espoused by radical advocates of 'public choice'. One extreme – state regulation and centralization – sometimes provoked another – radical deregulation and the loss of essential state regulatory functions. The abolition of special licences, quotas and trade privileges does away with an important source of corruption and economic distortion, yet the state's regulatory role could not be entirely eliminated.

These are some of the elements of postcommunist economic reform. The debate over the most appropriate pace and scale of changes has dominated discussion. According to Kaminski, for example, countries that were fortunate to have found leaders able quickly to force through the required changes and to withstand bitter domestic opposition fared better than those that accommodated the opposition or that sought some relatively painless 'third path'.[18] Yet there were often good reasons to adopt a more measured pace, including the elementary democratic practice of taking into account the views of elected representatives, who in Ukraine and elsewhere have opposed radical reform. Thus the dilemma has been not only over the speed of reform but also over its form. In Russia a relatively authoritarian approach was taken, including the marginalization of parliament, while in Ukraine a more conciliatory approach was adopted by both the first postcommunist president, Leonid Kravchuk, and the second (since 1994), Leonid Kuchma. The results, however, appear to speak for themselves. Poland witnessed strong growth after 1992, with Polish gross domestic product by 1996 reaching its 1989 level. For different reasons Slovakia has also registered strong growth since 1995. Hungary and the Czech Republic, too, appear to have turned the corner, while the economies of the three Baltic states have to differing degrees also begun to recover. The economies of most members of the Commonwealth of Independent States (CIS) continue to languish, although in places where the falls were most severe (Georgia, Armenia), some recovery has taken place. The stubborn failure of the Russian economy to move out of recession, and Ukraine's continued depression, however, prompted many to suggest that at some point Russia had taken a fundamentally wrong turn, allowing a criminalized oligarchy to hijack the reform process and then to impose its will on the country. Such views leave out of account the enormous progress (in strictly transformative economic terms) that has taken place. By the late 1990s Russia had become in essentials a market economy, subject to all the vicissitudes typical of a country integrated into the global capitalist economy. While what Jowitt dubbed 'hustler capitalism'[19] is certainly well entrenched and coexists with legal economies, there have been effective moves to liberal capitalism in a number of countries. What this brief survey of the economic dilemmas facing postcommunist countries suggests is that there is no single optimal approach to economic reform, yet certain fundamental principles are universal to them all. It is the balance to be drawn between specificity and universality that is the test of the leadership of each country: postcommunism once again demonstrates that it is in politics that economic problems are resolved.

Democratic transition

More has been written on postcommunist democratic transition than on any other aspect of the great changes of this period, and we can do no more than hint at some of the issues involved.

What definition of democracy should be applied? Most authors have adopted a minimalist procedural conception of formal democracy, characterized above all by the regular holding of competitive elections where there are few impediments to popular participation. The formal aspects of democracy have by and large been introduced in the Eurasian postcommunist societies, and this is by no means a small achievement, but while free and fair elections are certainly a necessary component of democracy, they are certainly far from sufficient. In many countries, in particular in the CIS states, parliaments have limited powers and there are few restraints on the prerogatives of the executive. As for more substantive issues of participatory and social democracy, these tended to be discredited by the communist failure to incorporate safeguards into their version of commune democracy. The alternative 'anti-political' strand in dissident political thinking that stressed the creation of independent organizations in the community has largely withered

away. Ideally, it might have been thought, some combination of
the actually existing substantive democracy (in the form of soviets
and their equivalents), the liberal principles of formal democracy (checks and balances, the separation of powers), and the
self-organization of society might have allowed postcommunist
societies to enjoy the best of all worlds, but nowhere have there
been experiments with new forms of democracy. On this terrain
postcommunist political development has proved resolutely sterile.
There has been little creative thinking on the relationship between
democracy and the market, and everywhere political and economic
élites have dominated while popular pressure and its organizations
have tended to be marginalized.

Just how liberal are these societies? In his survey of the 'anti-
political' thinkers of the 1980s, Jerzy Szacki argued that these indi-
vidualistic thinkers stressed human and civil rights but they failed
to engage with the classical liberal agenda of 'positive' liberal rights
such as freedom of speech. For him, political (as opposed to economic) liberalism was a shallow phenomenon, sustained earlier as
the discourse of the struggle against communism but lacking
authentic roots in the societies themselves.[20] Despite his rather pes-
simistic assessment, survey evidence suggests that political liberalism has a more solid basis in these societies than he allows. The
emphasis, nevertheless, since the fall of communism has been to
establish the material framework for commitment to the new order.
Above all, the policy of economic liberalism devised privatization
strategies to create a class with a vested interest in preserving the
new order. The definition of material interests, however, is impre-
cise, ranging from the attempt simply to keep one's job, earning div-
idends on a small packet of shares, to the enormous wealth of the
postcommunist oligarchs. Privatization in practice reinforced both
the horizontal and vertical segmentation of society, suggesting a
fundamental incompatibility between the programme and the
context.

While there are many examples of capitalist societies that are not
democratic, one would be stretched to think of a case where the
reverse is true. The relationship between democracy and the
market in postcommunist societies remains open although not
open-ended.[21] While political liberals tend to be economic liberals,
the reverse relationship is not always evident. The strategy of
market-oriented authoritarianism remains an important option,

especially in those countries where the economic upturn was delayed. The social basis for authoritarian modernization, unlike Taiwan and South Korea and even more a Chilean Pinochet-type solution, is more fragmented and the international climate since the end of the cold war is certainly not (yet) conducive to this outcome. Marketization itself, however, often appeared to represent liberation from the tutelage of the state and became the substitute for a more developed programme of political liberalism. In postcommunist countries the prior fusion of polity and economy set up a very different socio-structural dynamic than in other regions (for example, the post-colonial world), where élites benefited from independence. Capitalism itself became a new form of utopia, whereas for many of the post-colonial states it was identified with the colonial oppression from which they sought to escape. In postcommunist countries there is no traditional upper class enjoying economic rights nor a technocratic anti-democratic élite (as in Japan). Democracy and marketization are the fundamental bases of the legitimacy of the postcommunist regimes, whereas liberation and development were at the core of the self-identity of post-colonialist systems. In countries where the colonial experience was more distant, as in Latin America, there was no need for more marketization at the moment of transition, but in postcommunist countries the development of a non-state sector was at the very heart of the process. In short, the postcommunist context favoured a liberal economic paradigm, but tempered by social and other concerns.

In China the tension between democracy and the market appeared in a distinctive form. How compatible was a liberalized market economy with the maintenance of Communist Party rule? Rising unemployment, huge population movements, enviromental degradation, and growing disparities between the coastal regions and the hinterland could put the whole system under intolerable strain. The regime, however, did have resources in reserve: a high savings rate, a supportive diaspora, a disciplined and educated labour force and the development of a social welfare system distinct from the enterprises. Above all, the 58 million-strong Communist Party remained the core of a political system that was both robust and adaptible. The Party's general secretary, Jiang Zemin, began to introduce some limited democracy within the Party at its Fifteenth Congress in September 1997, with quaintly termed 'exceed-quota' elections offering some limited choice in elections

to the Central Committee. It was with reforms like this that
Gorbachev's *perestroika* had begun.

Constitution-making was the heart of the first phase of democratization. Elster noted the contrast between 'reason' in the
process, concerned above all with an impartial assessment of the
public good, and 'passion', derived from either past concerns or
contemporary interests pursuing sectional, institutional or personal
advantages.[22] No postcommunist country could avoid the tension
between reason and passion, especially since in Eastern Europe the
continental model of a *Rechtsstaat* constitution as the rigid codifi-
cation of fundamental laws was adopted. In Ukraine it took until
June 1996, and in Poland until May 1997, for new constitutions to
be adopted, while in Russia the process became bound up with the
intense conflict between the Soviet-era parliament and the presidency in the shape of Boris Yeltsin that exploded in military conflict in October 1993, and only in December of that year was a new
constitution in effect imposed in a plebiscite. As the fundamental
law, these constitutions not only dealt with the main political institutions and with basic human rights and freedoms, but also established who 'the people' would be, the nature of the state (federal
or unitary), the state language and the status of secondary lan-
guages, and the gamut of social rights.

The long debate between the relative merits of presidential and
parliamentary forms of government has been conducted with
renewed vigour in the postcommunist context. Since the onset of the
Jacksonian era in the United States in 1828, the president has been
perceived as the only representative of the people as a whole, and
strong echoes of the president as the voice of the people and a coun-
terweight to the vested interests represented in parliaments have
echoed throughout the postcommunist world, even in parliamentary
systems where the powers of the president are limited and formal.
The general tendency was for Central and Eastern European countries to adopt parliamentary systems, while the CIS states took the
presidential path. The very exigencies of transition appeared to
confirm the latter choice where the initiative for reform tended to
come from the presidential branch. The political implications,
however, were clear. In Russia, for example, the presidency was to
a degree above the separation of powers, combining certain judicial
powers with legislative functions in addition to the conventional
executive role. In presidential systems the parliaments were viewed

in a peculiar schizophrenic light: on the one hand, their legitimating role, their ability to broker compromises, to foster party systems and to oversee the legislative process was accepted; on the other, they were often viewed as obstructive of reforms, prolonging the travails of economic transition and giving voice to the worst forms of rejectionist, populist and xenophobic feelings that were deeply embedded in these traumatized societies.

The parliamentary systems of Central and Eastern Europe, however, were not immune to some of the problems faced elsewhere. The Czech Republic was long considered one of the most stable and economically successful countries until in late 1997 it became clear that the Thatcherite government, long headed by Václav Klaus, was embroiled in dubious party financial affairs, leading to the fall of his administration. The economic record of his government, moreover, was discovered to be built on shaky foundations. In Slovakia, as in some of the former Yugoslav states, new forms of authoritarianism emerged, despite the presence of popularly elected parliaments. Here the transition from communism to nationalism was seamless. The prime minister up to September 1998, Vladimír Mečiar, pursued an idiosyncratic mix of nationalism and economic liberalism. His feud with the former president of the republic, Michal Kováč, would be farcical if it were not so tragic. Slovakia was removed from the front ranks of countries lined up to join Western European institutions, above all the EU and the North Atlantic Treaty Organisation (NATO). Romania, however, after a period of quintessential postcommunism where it was difficult to distinguish where the old ended and the new began, from 1996 made rapid strides towards achieving the formal requisites of democracy. In the early years under president Ion Iliescu governments were dominated by the Party of Social Democracy, but spurred on by the prospect of NATO membership and the election of a new president in November 1996 (Emil Constantinescu) an accelerated reform programme sought to make up for lost time, although governments remained unstable. The ability of regimes to change fairly rapidly suggests that explanations of the diverging pattern of political development in different countries based on political culture need to be treated with care.

Romania (like Bosnia, Lithuania, Moldova, Poland, Russia and Ukraine) is an example of a semi-presidential system, where the president is elected for a fixed term and has more than ceremonial powers, while the prime minister must (effectively) maintain the confidence of the legislature. Such mixed systems are prone to conflict, although in some countries there is a clear (although not always stable) delineation of the respective powers. Bosnia is a special case, but in Russia and Ukraine the potential for conflict remains strong. Elsewhere, presidents have resolved conflicts with the legislature by extralegal means (Armenia, Croatia, Kazakhstan and Serbia, countries marked by a shift towards authoritarianism).[23] It is clear that some institutional configurations promote democratic conflict resolution, whereas others stimulate tensions between the various branches of government.

Belarus moved from a parliamentary to a presidential system and enjoys the dubious distinction of being the first European post-Soviet state to have regressed towards a form of plebiscitary authoritarianism. Lukashenka, the former manager of a collective farm, ran the country like an extended version of a peasant community. The weak tradition of national consciousness allowed the regime to assume some of the features characteristic of sultanism: extreme patrimonialism, where the polity is considered the personal domain of the sultan; the fusion of the public and private spheres; government by the ruler according to unrestrained personal discretion; the absence of the rule of law; the absence of a guiding ideology; weak institutionalization; limited political pluralism and minimal popular mobilization; and little scope for legitimate opposition, resulting in violent overthrow becoming the only way to remove the leader.[24] These were the features of Ceauşescu's regime under communism, and the way Belarus and some other republics began to develop under postcommunism. In Uzbekistan, President Islam Karimov took advantage of the civil war in Tajikistan to undermine what little opposition there was and establish an authoritarian regime. The Central Asian states are particularly reminiscent of the fate of the post-colonial countries, where civil and inter-ethnic tensions allowed leadership cults to emerge as the societies themselves sank ever deeper into debt and economic stagnation.

At what point along the 'transition' can we say that a country has become 'democratic'? Two key questions establish the parameters of democratic consolidation: are the institutions in place; and are the democratic reforms irreversible? The central question is the degree to which a functional set of institutions can be established that are independent of personalities. In Russia and some other

countries much still depends on individual relationships and the
struggle between powerful oligarchic groupings: power relations
remain negotiated rather than regulated by a set of impersonal
norms. Third-party adjudication and rule enforcement remain
weak in systems still characterized by the rule of individuals rather
than the rule of law. In most countries, however, constitutional
orders were established enshrining the separation of powers,
however rudimentary and unbalanced, that had an evolutionary
potential. As for the question of irreversibility, there is no doubt-
ing the fragility of much that has been achieved in the sphere of
democratization, an insecurity of the foundations of democracy
that in general becomes more marked the further east one goes.

State reconstitution

The dissolution of communist party power in Europe took place
too quickly to allow the states to reconstitute themselves on traditional lines. All postcommunist states suffered from governmental weakness, including to varying degrees difficulty in
collecting taxes and imposing the rule of law. In China, where the
Communist Party is gradually disengaging from the state, corruption is rife, the judicial system is weak and regional authorities are
asserting themselves against the centre. Elsewhere in Asia corruption undermined the rudimentary systems of financial market regulation, discouraged foreign direct investment and contributed to
the financial crisis from late 1997.

The majority of the 27 Eurasian postcommunist countries under-
went state reconfiguration in addition to the other traumas of the
transition. Only five survived in their original form: Albania, Bulgaria, Hungary, Poland and Romania. All the rest, to varying
degrees, were forced to reconstitute an administrative apparatus to
govern an independent state, although the 'continuer' states (Czech
Republic, Russia and Serbia) in possession of the capitals of the old
states had an immeasurable advantage over those forced to start
from scratch. Uninterrupted independent statehood was obviously
an advantage for some states, even if that state (like Hungary)
claimed to represent a larger nation. The Central Asian republics
had never enjoyed statehood in anything like their present configurations and, in addition, their rudimentary stateness was fragmented by clan, regional and ethnic loyalties that aggravated the

problem of creating new political communities. The identity of the new states was challenged by domestic and foreign élites, while the issue of borders (both the actual line and, in the case of the CIS states, their policing) remained contested.

Although by no means all the problems of postcommunist societies are a result of the past, with the policies adopted since the fall of the communist regimes themselves in many cases exacerbating the difficulties, the legacy was genuinely heavy. In the earlier system there was little differentiation between the economic and political spheres and thus postcommunist governments almost everywhere sought to liberate the economy from state administration through accelerated privatization and various forms of economic liberalization. Although privatization has too often taken the form, in common parlance, of 'piratization' by élites strategically placed to take advantage of the rich pickings from the sinking ship of state socialism, the underlying logic of disbursement appears to be inescapable. The role of the state appears to have been discredited (a theme we shall return to in Chapter 6), although even the World Bank shifted its stance to acknowledge the role of the state in the development and modernization of countries, in particular in the emergence of the Asian 'tiger economies'.[25] On its own, disbursement by no means guarantees the emergence of a rational and functioning market system or a more functionally limited state administration. In fact, the Russian state apparatus ballooned and by the late 1990s employed more functionaries than the old Soviet state which governed a much larger country with twice the population.

Albania demonstrates the failures of state construction. Dominated by a particularly corrupt postcommunist élite in which the business and political class was largely indistinguishable and presided over by President Sali Berisha, the whole system disintegrated in 1997 under the impact of failed pyramid investment schemes. The communist regime of Enver Hoxha had stifled the emergence of even the glimmerings of a civil society, of any social group that could carry the burden of the democratization project. It fell to the former communists in the Socialist Party led by Fatos Nano, and his successors, to begin to try to reconstitute some sort of political order. In a broader perspective, the secular nation-state was the product of a particular evolution of Western Europe, and there is no reason to assume that it must be the universal form for human community. Already we have seen the tension between the supranationalism of Islam and the states within which it was constrained following the fall of the European empires; and in Africa Robert Jackson has identified what he calls 'quasi-states', entities sustained less by stable relationships between the polity and society than by the conventions of the international system.[26]

Social reinvention – civil society resurgent

The collapse of state socialism appears to vindicate the anti-totalitarian 'civil society' approach to social theory. Quite apart from the obvious morbidities of 'civil society against itself', represented by inter-ethnic strife, corruption and criminality, the evolution of the social role of the concept of civil society in the last decades represents, in a profound sense, a fundamental re-evaluation of the role and scope of politics in modern society. As Gleason puts it: 'The triumphant recovery and idealization of the term "civil society" is only one dimension of the widespread notion that the world cannot be reformed, perhaps cannot even be improved, without an unacceptable risk of tyranny'.[27] The state could no longer be trusted either as the organizer of modernization or as the carrier of a broader social project like equality, and thus it fell to the task of society to take up the burden. But could postcommunist societies bear the load?

We have noted earlier (Chapter 2) how the concept of civil society was turned against the regimes – as a form of resistance for society to transcend communism even while formally still in thrall to its institutions. In the 1980s the concept appeared to represent a path towards the self-liberation of society, and ultimately a way of ensuring the state's accountability to society. Hannah Arendt's totalitarian thesis and George Orwell's *1984* were challenged by the fall of these allegedly immutable totalitarian systems, yet they have at the same time been substantiated by the rise of the civil society counter-movements to the aspiration of state socialism to 'control everything'. In the postcommunist era a distinctive Tocquevillian approach is adopted, focusing on the need for strong independent associations to stand between the state and the individual. This has been a two-edged process, allowing on the one side the emergence of civil associations, entrepreneurialism, philanthropy, organized religion, media diversity and so on, but, on the other, allowing the luxuriant flourishing of social morbidities, crime, corruption, poverty, drastic inequality, racism and ethnic conflict. Both processes represent in different forms the revenge of society on the state.

In Czechoslovakia, and later in the Czech Republic, Klaus's neoliberal economic evangelism had long put him at odds with the president, Havel, who continued to represent the 'anti-political' values of the old dissident movement. Their differences focused on differing evaluations of the role of civil society under postcommunism. For Havel, civil society represented the kernel of an alternative emancipatory social process, whereas Klaus would have none of this and lauded instead the anonymous operation of the market. The transition from dissent to government for Havel was clearly a personal drama of the very highest order, one that he came to terms with by eloquently articulating the view that dissent under communism helped preserve values that Western societies had themselves abandoned. These values focused on the existential relationship between the individual and the community, where personal self-discovery is part of the larger civilizational web of society.[28] The struggle against communism itself had generated a normative notion of civil society as the embodiment of an 'anti-political' autonomous and ethically charged arena based not on law but on trust and morality. Postcommunism not only did away with the legacy of communism but Havel's morality of 'living in truth', too, was lost. The anti-political notion of civil society as a moral order met the harsh realities of establishing a material order that could sustain the economic bases of civil society.

The affinities between postcommunist and precommunist societies have been noted before, but this is particularly striking in the social make-up of these societies. Postcommunist societies are characterized by pre-modern ethnic and territorial cleavages and stratification rather than the complex socioeconomic and interest cleavages of (post)modernity. If in the past parties tended to represent identifiable objective interests, such as the landed gentry or the industrial working class, now with fragmented societies in which the economic interests of the population were diffuse and depoliticized, while those of the élite were crudely direct and prepolitical, the role of political parties appeared redundant. With the decline of ideological politics classic lines of party affiliation were blurred, and parties had an inexorable tendency to become diffused into 'movements' and 'fronts', in which new forms of opinion and power were directly aggregated rather than mediated through a party hierarchy and organization. This is a universal phenomenon, applying as much to the former communist states as to others.

At the same time, although social variegation was distinctive, the social structure of communist (and thus of postcommunist) societies was far from undifferentiated, both within each country and between states. This means that we have to be sensitive to the particular social traditions of individual postcommunist countries, and above all have to be aware that there were well-defined and, sometimes, well-organized 'interest groups' in postcommunist societies that interacted with the transition process in a variety of diverse ways. Both as 'interests' and as 'groups' they were unusual, often locked into administrative relationships left over from the old regime or sustained by the informal clientilistic networks that had become so prevalent as communism decayed. Above all, it is clear that the communist regimes that had allowed elements of a 'parallel polis' (a type of second society) to develop contained the embryo of a civic culture and alternative élites who could help structure postcommunist politics even if they were not the immediate beneficiaries of the fall of the old system.

The threat of a populist reaction to the globalizing agendas of postcommunist governments was a real one. Indeed, Mečiar's government in Slovakia until its electoral defeat in September 1998, represented a type of populism in power, resentful of the West, intolerant of its minorities and jealous of its past. Populism as a matter of principle is anti-liberal, tending to reject the city as a source of foreign corruption. Above all, it is sometimes suggested that many of the same conditions that provoked the rise of the Nazis in Germany have emerged in some of the postcommunist countries. Many feel a sense of national humiliation and look for a scapegoat. In Russia numerous neo-fascist groups emerged, and anti-Semitic attitudes have even been voiced by some regional leaders. The combination of nationalist appeals for self-affirmation and the socialist promise of social security looked attractive for many, but already in 1993 the 'red–brown' coalition proved politically inept and adventuristic, and at no time did the extreme right gain more than an insignificant share of the vote – support for Vladimir Zhirinovskii's Liberal Democratic Party of Russia tended to reflect his personal vote rather than a right-wing agenda as such.

In Romania there were numerous neo-fascist parties, in the Czech Republic Miroslav Sladek's Republican Party made life difficult for Havel, while in Hungary Istvan Czurka's Justice and Life Party entered parliament for the first time in the 1998 elections.

The emergence of civil society without democracy represents a distinctive postcommunist inflexion of modernity. Democracy is usually the outcome of social development and antecedent cultural evolution yet, as with market reform, we are once again confronted by a giant bootstrapping operation in which decisions on what is desirable precede the cultural and institutional matrix that can sustain the choice. This is a logical absurdity since democracy is assumed to deal with decisions at the level of everyday reality, but it cannot be a method for imposing itself on a society by an act of human will. Thus democracy should be seen in its institutional and cultural context and not imposed as a universal for humanity as a whole. From this perspective postcommunist democratization becomes an overdetermined superideological normative project. From the liberal perspective democracy is an abstract but universal ideal, but for a variety of reasons not all societies can share in this bounty ('many are called, but few are chosen'), thus a hierarchy of states is established with the democratic states themselves establishing the hierarchy that places them firmly at the top. The suggestion made by Ernest Gellner that the term 'civil society' should be used in preference to 'democracy' suffers from a similar problem.[29] If one concedes a pluralism of political forms, why not a variety of cultural orders, some of which might find the notion of civil society antithetical?

Party formation

There are three main approaches to the study of the traumas of postcommunist party development: the *social structural* focuses on social cleavages, above all those of class, gender, religion and region; the *psychological* examines attitudes towards party identification and the filiation of ideological support; while the *historical* examines issues of 'repartification' (the reconstitution of precommunist parties) and the anti-party bias in societies stifled for so long by one-party systems. In Central Europe and Slovenia relatively stable party systems did emerge, while elsewhere the proliferation of parties by no means signalled the creation of viable parties, let alone the emergence of a hegemonic party as occurred in Italy, India and Japan. In presidential systems parties in parliament were estranged from the operation of government and, quite simply, had little positive to do, confirming all the worst prejudices against presidential systems.

In Russia the nascent party system was shaped by both the Soviet legacy and the informal movement origins of most parties. In the Soviet period the Communist Party had in effect merged with the state to form a party-state. Now, state-like parties emerged focused on acquiring influence within state structures, often with the view to colonizing some branch of administration or the institution of the legislature itself. In other words, rather than establishing a mass base below, parties focused their activities on establishing some vertical linkage above. The Communist Party of the Russian Federation (CPRF), as the main successor party in the country, was particularly prone to this, ensconcing itself in the Duma and, paradoxically, becoming, despite itself, one of the main supports of the system imposed after October 1993, inhibiting the emergence of destabilizing outsider groups of radical nationalists or democrats. The gulf between the so-called 'party of power' and the communist opposition at times narrowed almost to invisibility. A similar tendency was at work in Ukraine where the revived Communist Party led by Petro Simonenko became one of the strongest in the Verkhovna Rada.

Everywhere the postcommunist era is characterized by challenges to traditional parties and party systems as, for example, the media begins to act as the substitute for authentic political discourse and the old cleavages of class and the grand ideologies of the past give way to post-industrial concerns over imaging and the quality of life. This universal of postcommunism is particularly acute in the former communist countries. Although in many countries attempts were made to engineer electoral systems that would encourage political consolidation and the emergence of cohesive broadly based parties, on its own constitutional manipulation was not enough. Political parties in modern democracies are meant to perform several functions, but above all to *mobilize* support for relatively coherent programmes, to *represent* the needs and interests of civil society, and to *articulate* a vision of national purpose. In many postcommunist societies the relatively forced nature of the tasks of the transition promoted programmatic convergence and the inability to sustain coherent alternatives, while the relative weakness of interest differentiation in civil society and the narrowness of the range of the national purpose all conspired to inhibit the development of strong forward-looking parties. Party politics tended to focus on strong leaders and eclectic if not retrograde programmes, giving rise to the impression that much of what passed for party-political activities was no more than a mimetic substitute for authentic political life.

National reconfiguration

The collapse of the Soviet empire suddenly threw sovereignty into the ring, and the fruits of an independence that had hardly been desired let alone fought for fell to those already well placed when the music stopped. In the South Caucasus there were much stronger traditions of statehood (Armenia and Georgia, indeed, had been independent in the early Soviet years), but here, too, conflicts over territory, resources and borders exacerbated what were already severe economic crises. In Central Asia the situation more closely approximates the post-colonial countries of Africa, where 'lines drawn in the sand' reflected neither historical realities nor ethnic divisions. In the former Yugoslavia the separation of mixed populations into 'nation' states provoked Europe's first war since 1945.

Not surprisingly, postcommunism has been marked by a boom in nationality studies, yet certain basic conceptual issues remain unresolved. What is the relation of the nation to the state? To what extent is *some* sense of national identity a prerequisite for democracy? But how much is too much, and when does affirmative state-building nationalism (Ukraine) turn into negative state-destroying nationalism (Serbia)? Was the emergent authoritarianism in Belarus provoked by the country's weak sense of national identity, or was nation formation itself held back by an élite who preferred the chimera of Slavic Union and the retention of much of the old economy as part of a cynical attempt to retain power?

Political nationalism can be distinguished from ethnic nationalism. While the nationalism of the nation-state is on the wane (with some notable exceptions, such as Croatia and Serbia), the nationalism of ethnic groups is at an unprecedentedly high level. Ethnonationalism, as the latter is called, seeks to strengthen the identity, language and culture of a particular ethnic group, and usually to achieve some sort of administrative autonomy for it, whereas the political nationalism of the state is constrained by the growing web of globalizing and universalizing processes. The literature is divided between two broad approaches to modern national identity. The first is the 'primordialist' view, arguing that identity arises out of permanent features such as religion, language and customs. The corollary for primordialists is the tendency identified by Carlton Hayes, namely the aspiration to fulfil the principle of 'one nation, one state'.[30] The second 'modernist' view insists that nationalism is 'the pathology of modern developmental history', as Tom Nairn put it.[31] Gellner argued that it is created by modernization and the broadening of politics to encompass a mass element and acts to integrate societies challenged by the passage into modernity.[32] At the heart of Gellner's modernist definition is the desire to achieve congruence between state and nation, between state borders and cultural frontiers. While nationalism can be interpreted as a response to the traumas and stresses provoked by the industrial revolution, it can also represent a reaction to the fears and stresses engendered by the transition from traditional to modern life. The modernist position, however, underestimates traditional forms of collective identity. Anthony Smith has stressed that although nationalism is a modern phenomenon, it relies on pre-modern historical traditions and identity formation.[33]

Institutionalists take a distinctive approach to nationalism. Mancur Olson notes that nationalism

> is often not a pre-existing primitive belief to which other forces adapt – it is often a consequence rather than a first cause of political outcomes. As often as not, it is governments that create nationalisms rather than nationalisms that create nation-states . . . Even a language is, as the saying goes, usually a dialect backed by an army . . .[34]

Rebellious collective action in the former Soviet republics was possible, according to Olson, because there were already selective incentives promoting it, above all, people staffing an embryonic state.[35] Rogers Brubaker has developed these ideas, with the central notion of 'nationalizing states', regimes that have a state and then seek to paint it the colour of the ruling nation.[36] This is misleading in that it assumes a stark distinction between civic and ethnic models of nation building, whereas most lie at different points along a continuum. Ukraine, for example, is certainly involved in a complex process of nation building in the territory it inherited from the Soviet Union, and although there is a strong 'Ukrainizing' process at work, this does not necessarily threaten the quarter of the population that are not ethnically Ukrainian. Any reasonably effective nation-building process requires a national element, but this does not necessarily have to take nationalistic, let alone 'nationalizing', forms. Although clumsy, the distinction between 'nationalism' and 'nationism' might be useful here, with the latter signifying the creation of a supraethnic national identity that might be recognizably Russian, Ukrainian or whatever, but not drawn from one ethnic group alone.

Ethnic nationalism is inhibited (although by no means denied) by the globalizing and universalizing processes at work today. Romania's aspirations, for example, to join the EU and NATO prompted it to sign a friendship treaty with Hungary, while Russia's bid to join international economic and political bodies has so far restrained national revanchism. If this argument sounds familiar, it is of course the one advanced by liberals over the last 150 years. Economic liberalism was always associated with pacifism. As Carlton Hayes put it:

> Material economic conditions, [liberals] asserted, were far more decisive than mere political action; they were bound, in the new age, to assure the success of economic liberalism, to guarantee peace throughout the world, and to get rid of the excesses of nationalism.[37]

The First World War undermined the belief of both liberals and Marxists that nationalism was an archaic form of community that would give way to the transnational solidarities of capital or class.

The problem of minorities is by no means resolved, and the two cardinal principles of the Organization of Security and Cooperation in Europe (OSCE) – the right of national self-determination and the inviolability of borders – obviously (and painfully for Chechens, Kosovans and the Armenians of Nagorno-Karabakh) are contradictory. Postcommunist states have once again to establish the boundaries of the community: who is in and who is out. Are the Roma of Romania in, or the Hungarians of Transylvania and Slovakia, and what about the Turks of Bulgaria, the Uighurs of Xinjiang and the Tibetans in China? The very borders of some states remain contested: the Chechens, it appears, do not want to be part of the Russian political community, however democratic it might be, while the South Ossetians and the Abkhaz would consider their future more secure within the Russian Federation. The question concerns not only who are the people, but more particularly who are to be citizens, a problem particularly acute in Estonia and Latvia, where Slavic in-migration was used as an instrument of conquest (demographic imperialism) by the Soviet occupation regime, but where the individuals concerned (many of whom are now pensioners) cannot be held personally responsible. This is the type of problem in coming to terms with communism that we shall examine in the next chapter.

Democracy on its own is by no means the antithesis of nationalism; indeed, the opposite is often the case. The introduction of democratic proceduralism can act to empower nationalist mobilization, as took place in the former Yugoslavia. As Zakaria notes, 'without a background in constitutional liberalism, the introduction of democracy in divided societies has actually fomented nationalism, ethnic conflict, and even war'.[38] Drawing on Michael Doyle's view, lately restated in his *Ways of War and Peace* (1997),[39] Zakaria argues that it is not so much democratic states that do not go war with each other but states marked by constitutional liberalism: 'In countries not grounded in constitutional liberalism, the rise of democracy often brings with it hyper-nationalism and warmongering'.[40] This is an important corrective in the postcommunist context, where too often there has been excessive emphasis on abstract principles and processes of 'democratization' at the expense of framing constitutional orders appropriate to distinctive national conditions.

International reorientation – new states in a new order

What is the significance of the fall of communism for the international system? For Robert Cooper the event had an epochal meaning:

> 1989 marked a break in European history. What happened in 1989 went beyond the events of 1789, 1815 or 1919. These dates, like 1989, stand for revolutions, the break-up of empires and the re-ordering of spheres of influence. But these changes took place within the established framework of the balance of power and the sovereign independent state. 1989 was different. In addition to the dramatic changes of that year – the revolutions and the re-ordering of alliances – it marked an underlying change in the European state system itself.[41]

These changes, in his view, marked the end of the balance-of-power system in Europe, a paradigm shift in international relations comparable to the emergence of the modern European state system at the Peace of Westphalia in 1648. The old system is not simply being rearranged but a new system is emerging based on a new type of statehood where sovereignty is eroded by extension of the jurisdiction of normative processes, international courts, universal declarations, final acts and the like. The argument is not new but takes on a special urgency in the light of the changes after 1989. The very definition of statehood is indeed changing, with 'interference' in a state's domestic affairs taking on strengthened juridical forms. This is a process that I term *universalization* to distinguish it from the quantitive development of internationalization – a qualititative change is taking place where certain universal norms (dealing with issues such as human rights, environmental policy, trading regimes and financial systems) are agreed upon by bodies like the United Nations, the World Trade Organization and the International Criminal Court and then 'policed' in various ways. A universal 'policy state' (*Polizeistaat*) is emerging at the international level. Already the Helsinki Final Act had eroded the sovereignty of the communist systems, and their collapse in Europe later removed a major obstacle to the development of an era the first glimmerings of whose dawn we are now witnessing.

The onset of postcommunism was reflected in changes in the perception of geographical space. The term 'Eastern Europe' only gained general currency after the Second World War to represent the divisions of the cold war. The Austrian State Treaty of 1955 removed Vienna from 'the East' although geographically it is further East than Prague and, at the price of the neutrality of the country, allowed it to enjoy the fruits of the post-war economic prosperity of the West. Today there are growing links between countries on either side of the former Soviet border representing an expansion of the concept of Eastern Europe to include Ukraine, Moldova, Belarus and the Baltic republics. While the former northern tier Soviet bloc states (above all, Hungary and the Czech Republic) identify themselves as Central European states, for the former Soviet republics, recognition of their 'Eastern European' status marks an important step on their long journey to 'Europe'. Joint declarations between Poland and Ukraine signalled the end of centuries of suspicion, Poland and Lithuania regularized their relations and indeed began to develop a closeness that was reminiscent of the great days of the Polish-Lithuanian commonwealth, while Ukraine and Romania finally came to terms with the line of their border. The threat of conflict between the states of the 'new' Eastern Europe and the old was reduced, and by the same token the prospects for all to join the EU and NATO were enhanced. While Vietnam and Laos are still led by communist parties, the division of South-East Asia into communist and non-communist has far less importance than it once had. New sources of division are emerging, above all between archipelagic (Indonesia, Singapore, Malaysia, Brunei and the Philippines) and peninsular South-East Asia (Burma, Vietnam, Laos, Cambodia and Thailand).

While communist countries had been developing for various periods in one direction, the rest of the world had been moving at a furious pace in another. Under postcommunism the angle of re-entry for some countries proved easy, and indeed Poland, Hungary and some others had already anticipated their 'return to Europe'. For others, however, the change of course proved much more difficult to negotiate. How could Russia 'return to Europe' when it had always had an ambivalent relationship with the rest of the continent?[42] Foreign policy orientations changed dramatically, focusing on the question: who are our friends, who are our enemies, and who is the 'other'? Despite its own struggle against the legacy of communism, this for many countries appeared to be Russia itself. One of the reasons for the divergent characteristics of postcommunism in Eastern Europe and in the former USSR is that in the latter 15 states emerged out of one. The 'post-imperial' legacy is here particularly acute, not only because of the usual resentments generated by the colonial relationship but also by the very doubts over whether this was an empire at all. For Russia this is a time of retreat, but for the other 14 states a time of liberation. The dynamics of the situation are opposed, raising the question of the degree to which we can reduce very different experiences to a single dimension.

The end of the cold war endowed the international system with a new fluidity. The fall of the Berlin Wall was followed on 2 February 1990 by De Klerk lifting the ban on the African National Congress (ANC) and other restricted organizations, including the South African Communist Party. According to Giliomee, the changed international environment encouraged the ANC to abandon its revolutionary struggle,[43] while the end of the cold war allowed the ANC to be seen as a purely internal actor and no longer part of the global struggle against communism. The nature of the conjunction, however, needs to be examined. Guelke formulates the problem as follows: 'Was it simply coincidence that the two sets of events occurred together or were both products, at least in part, of change within the international political system itself?'[44] Techno-logical change, energy crises and the emergence of global markets threatened communist systems, the apartheid regime and other forms of authoritarianism alike. For Fukuyama the answer was clear:

> If there is any single answer to the question of why South Africa is moving toward full democracy at the beginning of the 1990s, it is because it, like the Soviet Union, China, South Korea, Brazil and Taiwan has gone through a period of authoritarian modernization that completely transformed the social and economic character of the country's elites.[45]

One might note that even countries like Zambia that had not undergone significant modernization were in the 1990s faced with the challenge of democratization. The replacement of the first generation of post-colonial leaders indicated the onset of a new era of post post-colonial politics in the region. At the same time, the systemic changes inaugurated by the end of the cold war acted as a slow-burning fuse that allowed dictatorships like that of Mobuto's in Zaire (now the Democratic Republic of Congo) to be over-thrown.

The signal feature of the reorientation of the international system after communism is that the new order was not renegotiated – the Western version was, in effect, imposed as the only viable option. Experience tells us that imposed orders are usually less stable than ones voluntarily agreed upon. The Second World War was not followed by a conference like that held in Vienna in 1815 or Paris in 1919, and once again the end of the cold war was not fol-lowed by a general debate about the principles of the new order. Havel noted that '[t]he old order has collapsed, but no one has yet created a new one', and warned:

> If the West, along with all the other democratic forces in the world, is incapable of rapidly engaging in the *common creation of a new order* in European and Euro-Asian affairs – a better order than the old bi-polar one – then someone else might well begin to do the job. . . .[46]

The concept of a postcommunist 'new world order' was first floated by George Bush in 1990 and then never developed, but it became the rallying point for opponents of the new configuration of international relations. Jowitt, along with many other others, inflected the notion to suggest a 'new world disorder'.[47] In Russia the 'new world order' took on the discursive role of the enemy of all progressive humanity once played by 'imperialism' and 'capitalism'. The CPRF's leader, Gennadii Zyuganov, used the notion as the centrepiece of his assault against the West and the malevolent plans of 'cosmopolitan' and Masonic circles to weaken and marginalize Russia – the coincidence of Bush's slogan and the Masonic inscriptions adorned by the announcement of a *Novus Ordo Seclorum* on dollar bills was proof enough of this! The wounded tone is captured by Henry Trofimenko's comment on American demands, following the exposure of Aldrich Ames, that Russia unilaterally expose any other spies: 'Evidently some people in the United States establishment are now confusing Russia with Puerto Rico'.[48]

Havel noted that the fall of communism caused the West 'some major headaches': 'After all, the world used to be so simple: there was a single adversary who was more or less understandable ... whose sole aim in its final years ... was to maintain the status quo. At the same time, this adversary drew the West together as well'.[49] With the end of the cold war the world has become a more dangerous place in two important respects. The conventions of the cold war and the dominance of the two superpowers limited nuclear proliferation and ensured control over the raw materials of nuclear weapons technology. Much of this has now gone, and in Russia there are serious concerns about the safety of its nuclear arsenal and stocks of weapons-grade fissile materials. Although Belarus, Kazakhstan and Ukraine joined the 1968 Non-Proliferation Treaty as non-nuclear states in 1992 and transferred their weapons to Russia, proliferation took a dangerous step forward with the explosion of nuclear weapons in India and Pakistan in May 1998. The second dangerous factor is the greater likelihood of regional wars with the end of cold war bloc discipline. The wars of Yugoslav disintegration would have been inconceivable during the cold war, while it is unlikely that Iraq would have risked invading Kuwait in 1990 if the USSR had still been a potent force. In Latin America the prospect of a regional arms race threatened the continent's

stability. Everywhere postcommunism coincided with and intensified challenges to the nation-state, above all from the forces of the
global financial economy.

There is no guarantee that liberal democracy will triumph from
Vladivostok to Vancouver. In the inter-war years democracy everywhere was in retreat when, as today, sectarian and often corrupt
politicians, disappointed populations and intransigent nationalities
sought solutions in authoritarian movements. The differences
between post-imperial and postcommunist Europe, however, are
striking. For all its faults, communism resolved some of the main
issues, above all the peasant question, and some problems of
development, although in turn it created different problems. The
end of the cold war put an end to bloc politics and provoked a
fundamental change in the international system while promoting
the (mainly Western) organizations that had structured the cold
war into permanent institutions of the postcommunist order. The
end of the constraints of the cold war endowed the international
system with a new fluidity, while in the domestic politics of countries such as Italy and Japan blockages on political development
were removed. For the Central European countries the 'return to
Europe' was less problematical although more drawn out than
anticipated, while for the rest polity issues had by the late 1990s
been largely resolved, although policy questions remained in flux.
In some countries the transition appears to be less from totalitarianism to democracy than from old to new dictatorship, but elsewhere democracies are becoming established.

Coming to Terms with Communism

The evaluation of the communist past is at the heart of both the universal and the specific strands of postcommunism. In the *annus mirabilis* of 1989 the long cold war, which in a conceptual sense began in the 1840s, between capitalism and communism came to an end. As Roberto Campos puts it: 'The latter ceased to be a paradigm. For some this is a nightmare, for others it is a source of nostalgia; but for no one is communism a model'.[1] He goes on to argue that 1989 will be seen as one of the great historical watersheds, 'comparable perhaps to 1776, when the great passage began from mercantilism to liberal capitalism and constitutional democracy'. He quotes José Merquior to the effect that, '[a]t the end of the 1940s, socialisms were in the role of judges, and in the 1980s in the role of "prisoners of judgement"'.[2] For Brzezinski 'communism will be remembered largely as the twentieth century's most extraordinary political and intellectual aberration'.[3] Coming to terms with communism means not only dealing with its consequences but perhaps above all understanding how the communist 'aberration' could have emerged out of the heart of the Western rationalist and Enlightenment traditions and then taken such morbidly violent forms in practice while in principle espousing emancipatory ideals.

Conscience, context and revolution

Transcending the communist past remains an ambiguous project; communism was more than a system of government but became part of the living texture of society itself. In Hungary Péter Esterházy noted: 'Even if it were true – which still must be proved – that the country shook off communism in 1956 as a dog shakes off water, today it is not at all clear where the dog ends and where the water begins'.[4] For most Eastern European states communism could at least be perceived as something imposed by an alien power, but in Russia no such easy way of coming to terms with the past was available. Communism became an indelible part of Russian history, marked by extremes of horror and achievement. Coming to terms with communism here would be exceptionally difficult, and (as in post-war Germany) profound processes of social amnesia, combined with the selective recovery of memory, helped the society cope with its current woes.

Not only postcommunist countries have to come to terms with communism, but also (and perhaps above all) the cultures that had given birth to the revolutionary socialist challenge. For Eastern Europe Marxian socialism was something imposed from the East, but for Russia it was an ideology imported from the West. David Caute long ago castigated much of the Western left for its acquiescence in Soviet crimes,[5] while in his introduction to *The Black Book of Communism*, Stéphane Courtois argues that Western European communists were morally complicit in the crimes committed in the name of their ideology in the East.[6] The condemnation of Western academics, especially the so-called 'revisionist' historians who from the late 1960s had rejected the concept of totalitarianism, became quite a cottage industry. They were accused of having been blind to the ills afflicting Soviet-type systems, above all overestimating the shift from 'totalitarianism' towards pluralism and exaggerating the socioeconomic successes of the regimes, and thus failed to predict their imminent demise. Such criticisms contain some truth, but in the larger context are fundamentally misconceived: it is not the job of social scientists to predict but to anticipate, and very few serious scholars failed to note the major problems facing communist systems. Even with the benefit of hindsight it is far from universally accepted, for example, that the nationalities question precipitated the fall of the Soviet Union; on the contrary, many would argue that the disintegration of the USSR was a far from inevitable consequence of the dissolution of the communist system.

More profoundly, was it not time to face up to the 'asymmetry of indulgence' (to use Ferdinand Mount's term)[7] whereby Nazism was cast out into the outer darkness of malevolence while communism became somehow a lesser evil. Courtois notes that communist regimes world-wide directly and indirectly claimed the lives of between 85 and 100 million individuals, at least double the number taken by Hitler.[8] According to him, 'terror was one of the inherent features of communist systems from the very beginning'.[9] Genocide 'of race' was now joined by genocide 'of class',[10] what I have called elsewhere 'classicide'.[11] Social category rather than individual innocence or guilt became the criteria for mass exterminations launched by communist authorities. How could such systems have retained their international legitimacy right to the end? And what about China and its enormous system of camps, the *laogai*, where, according to the dissident and former prisoner Harry Wu, as many as 50 million were incarcerated up to the mid-1980s and which still operate?[12] While there is now little doubt that quantitatively communism was responsible for more deaths than Nazism, the qualitative differences have long been debated. During the historians' debate (*Historikerstreit*) in the 1980s conservatives such as Ernst Nolte suggested not only comparison but also filiation: that Nazism itself was a response to the communist threat and Hitler learnt some of the techniques of mass murder from Stalin.[13] Courtois argues that no cause-and-effect relationship can be established between the coming to power of the Bolsheviks and the emergence of Nazism,[14] yet the cumulative effect of *The Black Book of Communism* and others of its genre is to relativize the Holocaust – that is, to 'historicize' it, to legitimate comparative methodology. Every death is unique, but the attempted mass extermination by production-line methods of an entire people is in a category of its own. Courtois comments on this as follows: 'After 1945 the genocide of Jews became the paradigm of modern barbarism, and occupied the entire space reserved for the perception of mass terror in the twentieth century'.[15]

Soon after the failed coup of August 1991 Alexander Yakovlev, Gorbachev's closest aide during the radical phase of *perestroika*, noted that Bolshevik communism 'lost its dispute with history'. Socialist society, according to him, could only have been 'post-bourgeois', not 'anti-bourgeois'.[16] While revolutionary socialism might have lost its dispute with history, the historicization of communism is itself a multi-faceted process. Historicization in this context means the relativizing of the communist challenge, depriving it of both its positive and its negative moral charge. Communism is thus relegated from a liberating movement to a failed experiment: it was not capitalism but communism that was consigned to the 'dustbin' of history, to borrow Trotsky's comment on the Provisional Government in 1917.

The historicization of Stalinism itself, and more broadly of the USSR in its entirety, provokes no less controversy than the Holocaust. Was the Soviet experiment a revolt against reason and the natural order of things, a utopia in power that dealt with human raw material as a forester treats wood (to use Stalin's aphorism: 'When wood is chopped, the chips will fly'), or was it just another species of modernity, a noble attempt to achieve collective values and to overcome historical backwardness and national weakness? The communist project never resolved the tension between politics and morality but today a new dilemma emerges: in evaluating communist systems, how can morality be combined with good history? It is over issues such as these that the 'asymmetry of indulgence' noted above comes into play: the USSR, after all, was part of the alliance that defeated Nazi Germany and sacrificed the most to achieve that victory; the USSR and China supported national liberation movements and, in particular, the Vietnamese war for the unification of the country; China for long claimed to represent the Third World, and communism in that country (and others) fulfilled vital national tasks, above all development, unity and stability; Communism was a positive ideal of human liberation whatever it might have turned into in practice, whereas fascism was always based on a vicious social Darwinist view of permanent struggle; many Western workers and intellectuals supported the communist ideal despite their tortured relationship with the country that claimed to represent its embodiment; and the sheer longevity of the Soviet system allowed generations to become accustomed to the polarity that it represented. There were positive elements in the communist past, although there is no consensus on what precisely the good bits were. Above all, in the final audit of the communist experience how can we balance the mountain of corpses against questionable achievements?

Communist regimes have to be judged in their historical context. A debate in Poland, for example, has sought to evaluate the record of the former regime.[17] While historical necessity after Yalta placed the country in the Soviet sphere of influence, there remained some room for manoeuvre. On the individual level it is clear that it took great courage for the Catholic journal *Tygodnik Powszechny* to refuse to print eulogies to Stalin on his death in March 1953 – and the paper's publication was suspended until 1956. On the national level, what did communism do for Poland? The country enjoyed an unparalleled period of peace and development, free from the fear of external invasion as long as the 'geopolitical fact' of subordination to Moscow was recognized. Culturally, the country developed enormously, with the achievement of near universal literacy, a hugely expanded higher education sphere and greatly reduced social inequalities. As for the economy, the record here as in most other communist countries is mixed. Compared with the inter-war years, the country made notable advances in industrialization, urbanization, health care and the provision of consumer durables. However, in comparison with countries at comparable levels of development such as Italy, Spain or Finland, Poland's development was less impressive and achieved at enormous environmental cost and waste. Above all, communism in Poland (and some other Eastern Central European countries), was perceived as anti-national and an instrument of subordination to a foreign and alien power. In Russia the developmental audit has been the subject of considerable controversy, especially since the figures themselves are contested. For Central Asia modernization came in a communist guise, and thus is far more deeply ingrained in the physical and mental fabric of these societies.

Communism might have lost its dispute with history, but much of its power derived from its seductive philosophy of history. In communist practice historical necessity manifested itself in the view that once the spirit and meaning of history was understood then certain sacrifices (both of oneself and – preferably – others) inevitably follow. Czesław Miłosz used the metaphor of the 'Hegelian bite' to describe those in post-war Poland who came under the spell of the mystique of historical necessity. The establishment of the Soviet-backed communist regime in the country was seen as progressive, together with its 'newthink' ideological certainties, however frequently they changed in detail. Jakub Karpinski noted that

> Marxism, as described in *The Captive Mind* [by Miłosz], is not a matter of purely intellectual considerations. It is a set of imprecise convictions, allowing for different imposed interpretations, ready-made for believers or for those pretending to believe. Some pretended so skillfully that they convinced themselves they did believe.[18]

The poet Zbigniew Herbert dispensed with Hegelian mystifications in explaining why some succumbed to the 'Hegelian bite' and reduced it simply to fear and bad faith. Karpinski sums up Herbert's view that 'it was not the mind that had gone wrong among Stalinist writers, it was character'.[19] This does not help explain the dilemma of genuine believers ('holy fools'?) in the new order willing to sacrifice themselves 'for the good of the cause'. Michnik notes that:

> We should remember that communism was not born in 1945 – or in 1939. We should take seriously the motives of those who believed in communism . . . The now widely held view that communism was nothing but the work of Soviet agents makes it impossible to understand the paths that people took to communism, the attractions of Communist ideology, and the experiences that led people to break with it.[20]

For many, he notes, communism represented an ideal of justice, and against the background of the inter-war failures and the rise of Nazism and Stalinism, gained strength from the belief that Western civilization had exhausted itself. Solzhenitsyn has a profound understanding of the dilemma of the 'honest communist', having written a novella entitled *For the Good of the Cause* in which the betrayal by the authorities of the idealism of the people is poignantly depicted,[21] and later given perhaps the best summary of the problem in which he combined the view that 'the line dividing good and evil cuts through the heart of every human being' with national repentence, self-limitation and what is today called 'sustainable development'.[22]

Miłosz and others, while no doubt right in the main, leave out of account something that is difficult to explain but undoubtedly important in countries emerging from the trauma of war and the endless disappointments of the inter-war years. Jan Jerschina puts this subjectivity as follows:

> The Poles, although often with pain in their hearts, did not want to fight any more. This 'recognition of reality' at this time was perhaps one of the reasons for the ease with which, during the next few years, Stalinism penetrated into the communal life of a great number of Poles. One normally speaks discreetly about 'war-weariness'. But it was not simply war-weariness: it was also a matter of a moral and political choice.[23]

Christa Wolf's *The Divided Heavens* (1963) describes the fate of a couple torn apart by the construction of the Berlin Wall in 1961,

while her *Thinking about Christa T.* (1968) is a remarkable study of
lost idealism. She was no dissident but neither was she a party hack,
creating space to preserve her integrity as a writer and a person; but
as someone who stayed in East Germany to the end (and beyond),
she became the object of vilification, often by West Germans who
had never faced the impossible choices forced upon intellectuals
(and, indeed, every honest citizen) under communism.

While the communist and Nazi crimes are obviously comparable
in scale, they are not commensurate. The difference lies not only
between genocide and 'classicide', the destruction of whole groups
on the basis of social criteria, important as these may be, but in the
fundamental orientations of the regimes themselves. While for the
Nazis economic growth served an ulterior purpose, the development of military power; in most communist countries economic
development itself became the purpose of the regime. In this
sense John Kautsky was right to argue that these regimes became
developmental societies and should be analysed with societies at
comparable levels of development.[24] The goals of the communist
movement, however much travestied in practice, were benign, and
thus the issues of conscience and natural justice emerge in a very
different light than in post-fascist societies. The USSR's role in the
defeat of Hitler as part of an alliance with the Atlantic states, with
the enormous sacrifices that this entailed, was not simply a tactic
for the self-preservation of the Stalinist ruling élite – although it was
certainly this as well.

Decommunization, expediency and natural justice

Although Lavrenty Beria and some other former leaders of the
People's Commissariat of Internal Affairs (NKVD) were shot after
Stalin's death in 1953, this was done mainly to protect the successors and had nothing to do with justice. The issue of destalinization,
formally opened in Khrushchev's 'Secret Speech' in February 1956,
is still far from over. Perhaps the central question was how a society
like Russia could live in peace with itself when it harboured thousands of individuals responsible for mass murder. They should at
least, it is argued, be banned from high office, otherwise the
integration of the old élite would incorporate the worst habits and
attitudes of the past, making a breakthrough into a genuine post-
imperial and postcommunist future, where human rights were

respected and the rule of law observed, that much more difficult. Unlike Germany or Japan, there were no victors from outside to impose retribution on a defeated regime, and instead it appeared that for the sake of an evolutionary transition to democracy forgiveness, but not forgetfulness, was the only appropriate response. Yeltsin's decree that the eightieth anniversary of the Bolshevik revolution on 7 November 1997 would become a day of 'Reconciliation and Concord' was greeted with incredulity by the neo-communists, yet the act sought to superimpose a new discursive formulation on the communist experience and thus, as it were, to expropriate history and to imbue it with a new meaning. Was this not a more effective way of coming to terms with the communist legacy than a generalized purge that would once again create a new class of victims, and thus perpetuate the very communist divisiveness that it sought to transcend?

Although at Nuremberg some of the leading Nazis were tried and condemned, denazification in Germany was soon abandoned as the cold war intensified. The symbolic point, however, had been made: the Nazi party had been a criminal organization and its activists were barred from serving the new republic or educating its citizens. Elsewhere in Europe only a few hundred officials and functionaries of those implicated in Nazi crimes were ever tried.[25] In France, belatedly, some of the collaborators of the Vichy regime were only taken to court in the 1990s. Continuity and stability, rather than prosecution and a thorough examination of the conscience of the nation, was the course chosen by post-war governments. Decommunization has typically taken a similar course. Postcommunism is torn over whether those who came to serve the new regime were self-deluded fools or self-serving villains. The great majority, of course, simply acquiesced. The debate over the communist past continues unabated. Tadeusz Mazowiecki, the first Polish non-communist prime minister, in his inaugural speech to parliament on 24 August 1989 promised to draw a 'thick line' (*gruba kreska*) under the past.[26] The crimes and betrayals of the past were to be forgotten and state–society relations were to begin anew, on a blank slate if not quite on a *tabula rasa*; the state promised to 'tell society the truth' and not to 'divide citizens into categories'. In Russia it is illegal to disclose information about KGB informants, a measure designed to prevent state security files becoming a weapon in political conflicts. But what about atonement for the crimes of the past?

The paradigm at work here on the whole is forgiveness and reconciliation in keeping with the 'anti-revolutionary' logic of the transcendence of communism. This is not cowardice but a positive emphasis on the normative character of the 'self-limiting' revolution based on an understanding that retribution generates new cycles of grievances.

This has not prevented calls, for example by the former dissident Vladimir Bukovskii, for new Nuremberg trials to judge the criminal activities of the Soviet regime. How this could avoid turning into a witch-hunt and a partisan political affair is not clear unless very clear guidelines were established from the outset. John Borneman has noted that public forms of retributive justice in postcommunist societies helped avoid spontaneous forms of retributive violence while promoting the principle of the accountability of public officials for acts of criminality.[27] But how far back should one go? In his study of the human rights abuses typical of communist governments and the policies adopted by the successor regimes to 'righting the wrongs' of the past, Istvan Pogany notes that the anticommunist regimes of the late 1930s were guilty of many human rights abuses themselves.[28] And what about those in Latvia and elsewhere who had collaborated with the Nazi occupiers in the extermination of the Jews? Commissions of Truth were established in some Latin American countries (Chile, El Salvador and Guatemala) and, as in South Africa with its Truth and Reconciliation Commission, amnesty laws were passed at the same time.[29] The human rights violations were investigated, but the perpetrators were promised immunity from prosecution if they gave full testimonies of their past (wrong)-doings.[30]

In October 1991 Czechoslovakia was the first to adopt a 'law on lustration' that banned citizens who had been active in the communist regime from holding office (lustration means spiritual or moral purification to remove bloodguilt). In 1992 the Polish parliament adopted a law on lustration, despite the opposition of Jacek Kuroń and other veterans of the dissident and Solidarity movement. One of the main problems with this and other lustration laws elsewhere was the verification procedure. A list of 64 high officials who had collaborated with the secret police was delivered in June 1992, and even Lech Wałęsa was named in a separate list. How could someone clear their name? What did collaboration in this context mean? The very heroism that prompted an individual to struggle against communism

might have forced them to enter into relations with the secret police
that would later expose them to charges of collaboration, while those
who quietly acquiesced under communism ('the prudent, with clean
hands', as Michnik terms them) could under postcommunism exult
in their moral superiority and demand 'cleansing' and strict decommunization. After the fall it was discovered that Christa Wolf had
been under Stasi surveillance since 1979, and in her file she was
identified as an *inoffizieller Mitarbeiterin* (unofficial informant), who
had allegedly appraised the 'class views' of other writers for the
secret police. The standard defence for this sort of 'collaboration' is
that the reports did not harm anyone, yet the question must be:
'What did you think you were doing when you made these reports?'
Only the unambiguous application of the rule of law, with the application of standard rules of evidence for those guilty of specified
crimes, could help the societies purge themselves of the past – for
the rest, let those without sin cast the first stone.

The issue is not only one of moral ambiguity but also a recognition of the complexity of communist reality. It became known, for
example, that most of the files of Securitate informers who were
Romanian Communist Party members were destroyed in the 1970s,
while another 27,000 files 'disappeared' from Securitate records
between 22 December 1989 and 26 March 1990, that is, after the
fall of communism.[31] The incomplete records would mean that
documentation would remain primarily only for the weak and unin-
fluential, who in any decommunization process would suffer yet
again. While no two cases are the same the following may be taken
as typical. In June 1998 the Romanian health minister, Francisc
Baranyi, was asked to resign when he admitted to having been
recruited as an informer 40 years earlier. He insisted that he was
forced to do so 'at gun point', and had never provided any information to the Securitate.[32] Eduard Shevardnadze, the former
Georgian interior minister, Soviet foreign minister and then from
1992 president of Georgia, added his voice to those opposed to the
opening of KGB archives of the Stalinist period and the publication
of lists of KGB agents. He argued that during the 70 years of communist rule 'tens of thousands' of people were forced to collabo-
rate with the KGB and opening the archives at this point, he
insisted, would provoke 'a new wave of resistance, mistrust and
hatred' and would 'reopen old wounds'.[33] Polish president Alek-
sander Kwaśniewski refused to condemn the communist past,

insisting that it was too complex to be encapsulated in one con-
demnatory sentence or paragraph: 'It was a period when some
people were loving one another, some were being held in prison,
some were working, and some were wasting their talents because
they had no possibilities for self-development'.[34]

While there were major problems with any generalized lustration
process, responsibility for specific crimes was another matter. The
creation of a new governing coalition following the September 1997
Polish parliamentary elections that included the right-wing Solidarity Electoral Action, together with the liberal Freedom Union,
prepared the way for renewed decommunization. Trials of communist officials responsible for the deaths of 44 workers in the
protests of December 1970 on the Baltic coast began in June 1998.
The complicity of the defence minister at the time, Wojciech
Jaruzelski, in these events was to be examined separately, while his
responsibility for the imposition of martial law in December 1981,
the suppression of the Solidarity movement and the associated
deaths, led to many calls for a full judicial inquiry, if not more.
Jaruzelski's assertion that his 'self-invasion' was designed to pre-
empt Soviet military intervention was contradicted by former
Soviet generals, who insisted that by December 1991 plans to intervene had been shelved. The lustration law adopted in April 1997,
despite the opposition of the then ruling Social Democrats, was
activated, obliging high public officials to declare whether they had
served in or collaborated with the communist secret police. On 18
June 1998 the Polish parliament passed a resolution condemning
the 'communist dictatorship imposed on Poland by force and
against the nation's will by the Soviet Union and Joseph Stalin', and
in particular held the Polish United Workers' Party responsible for
the 'many crimes and offenses' of the past.[35] The resolution, which
represented at least a slight vindication of those in the government
who had long struggled against the communist regime, reflected the
fact that decommunization could not be separated from short-term
political considerations and was used both to condemn the past and
to discredit contemporary political opponents.

Communists after communism

Postcommunist communism evolved in two directions. The first was
towards social democracy, with all of the dilemmas associated with

that, above all whether its purpose is to abolish the market or to humanize it. The other path is that of 'national communism', the option taken by Slobodan Milošević in Serbia, and favoured by Zyuganov in Russia. Earlier, national communism had been a viable option as long as it was defined against the 'hegemonic' tendencies of the Soviet Union, and was developed the furthest in Romania under Ceauşescu. Under postcommunism, however, national communism inexorably became communist nationalism; the power system of communism focused on a dominant party, mostly shorn of the fundamentals of Marxist-Leninist ideology, fused with an agenda of radical and mostly xenophobic nationalism. Under postcommunism the radical right and the radical left joined in their repudiation of modernity (individualism, role of markets, independent civic associations and parliamentarianism).

The return to power of postcommunist communists is sometimes misleadingly suggested to indicate the return of communism. Postcommunism has been marked by *social* compromises with the old élite, but this does not indicate a *political* compromise with the old regime. Communists, not communism, won elections in Lithuania, Bulgaria, Hungary and Poland. The return of communists to office is hardly surprising since they represented the largest pool of talent and experience. The great majority, moreover, did not place themselves outside the political mainstream but accepted the 'rules of the game' of the new democracies. Only a few parties became antisystem and on the whole they were marginalized. Indeed, the inclusion of the former communists and the successor parties into the new polities helped consolidate them while avoiding the creation of an excluded group committed to revenge. Richard Rose's study of what ex-communists think discovered that '[d]ifferences between countries are greater than differences between Communists and ex-Communists within one country'.[36] The majority of former communists considered party membership the price worth paying for career advancement and showed little residue of any ideological fervour that they might have had.

Communism as a *political* movement appears acceptable, but communism as a project is not. As Cotta notes on the basis of the success of the postcommunist parties in Poland, 'the political delegitimation of the communist regime no longer entails the delegitimation of the successor parties'.[37] It has been argued, moreover, on the basis of the Hungarian experience that the victories of the

ex-communists in 1993–94 'did not represent a lasting correction
from the ambitious changes of 1989–90, but a singular and temporary setback in the dismantling of the socialist value system'.[38] In
Central and Eastern Europe communists, who had spent their
entire existence fighting revisionism, now embraced social democratic reformism as a kindred movement. At its best communism
was a form of extended state welfarism, and now the postcommunist communist parties returned to their roots, before the fateful
rivalry between revolutionary and evolutionary socialism split
social democracy. Their aim now was to shell out the social democratic core from the revolutionary communist project, to sustain
some form of welfarism without the enormous bureaucracies of
state socialism. The failure of strong new social democratic parties
to emerge suggests that the former parties were successful not
because they were social democratic but because of their calls to
modify the allegedly extreme neo-liberalism of the first generation
of postcommunist leaders. When postcommunist 'communist'
parties came to power in Eastern Europe, however, they almost
universally failed to implement the radical social and democratic
proposals for which they campaigned when seeking office. Left
parties in power everywhere pursued right-wing policies. These
parties accepted the broad programme of liberal modernization,
albeit proclaiming their intention to soften the harder edges, and
thus placed themselves in the vanguard of the societies' hopes for
renewal and integration. They also placed themselves at the mercy
of the vicissitudes of electoral politics. The Lithuanian Democratic
Party of Labour suffered a severe defeat in 1996, while in the Hungarian elections of 1998 the Socialist Workers' Party was removed
from power. The Party of Democratic Socialism (*Partei des
Demokratischen Sozialismus*), the successor to the East German
Socialist Unity Party (*Sozialistische Einheitspartei Deutschlands*),
entered into the broader mainstream of German political life with
more effect than the old *Deutsche Kommunistische Partei* ever had
since the end of the war.

   In the former Soviet Union, however, communism retained
something of its old ferocity. The CPSU proved to contain its own
antitheses, but this antithesis was not only to the Soviet Communist Party in particular but to the whole trajectory of the communist
movement in general from its inception in the mid-nineteenth
century to at least Stalin. This antithesis was nationalism, now

counterposed to the internationalism of Marxian communism. The CPRF was paralysed by its internal disagreements and failed to renew itself either ideologically or organizationally, and by attempting to combine the nationalist and the communist traditions, failed to preserve either. Clearly, in the context of the dissolution of the world communist ideal, together with the disintegration of the international communist movement, communist parties have no alternative but to stress their national credentials. The roots of national communism, however, lie deeper – both fascism and communism have common roots in the stresses generated by the adaptation of traditional states to the challenges of modernity and modernization. At the same time, the CPRF's resort to populism was yet another sign of the breakdown of traditional class politics. The CPRF lacked a modernizing idiom in which to transform itself, and thus clung all the more to the symbols of socialism and the past, above all the restoration of the USSR. The CPRF's adoption of a nationalist agenda acted as the alternative to the modernization of the party itself and above all of society. As Jeremy Lester noted: 'No one has done more than Zyuganov to correlate *post*-communism with *pre*-communism'.[39] In Ukraine the Communist Party increased its representation in parliament in the 1998 elections, rising from 90 to 120 of the 450 seats, to a degree at the expense of its socialist peasant allies and predominantly concentrated in the Russophone East. The stalemate over economic reform looked set to continue. In Azerbaijan the old party boss, Heidar Aliev, was returned to power following the overthrow of the nationalist government of the Azerbaijan Popular Front in 1993, and he proceeded to accommodate the pluralistic electoral system to the realities of a quasi-authoritarian presidential regime.

The postcommunist epoch can really be reckoned to have begun when communists lost the will to power – power here defined as a monopolistic dominance over the institutions and processes of government. The CPRF, for example, no longer represented an anti-system opposition or even an anti-national one; it became, like many Western communist parties in the cold war era, both part of the system and opposed to it. The failure of the CPRF to make the social democratic turn, however, reflected its own organizational evolution and the broader context of Russian politics. While anti-communism was the corner-stone of Yeltsin's 1996 presidential campaign, its resonance is probably of limited political duration, playing almost no role in the regional elections from September 1996, and could be counter-productive in any future election. The question remained, however, whether the CPRF could be allowed to form the government, or its leader, Zyuganov, to become president. In 1996 the Russian financial and political élites, together with the majority of the population, appeared to answer in the negative: Russia's fragile democracy and nascent market economy would not be safe in communist hands. The situation is comparable to that found in Algeria in 1992, when the Islamic Salvation Front won the elections in a democratic ballot, but was then not allowed to take power. The consequence was the launching of a guerrilla war that claimed thousands of lives. With the experience of Weimar Germany and Hitler's rise to power, few would deny that democracies have the right to defend themselves, yet there is the opposite danger, that the very act of defending democracy may subvert it. The problem of achieving a mature political community in Russia, Ukraine and some other coutries is far from complete.

The collapse of communism saw radical changes in the non-ruling communist parties as well. In Italy the PCI split in 1990, with a fundamentalist successor party (*Rifondazione Comunista*, Communist Refoundation), and one (*Partito Democratico della Sinistra* (PDS), the Party of the Democratic Left) that built on the earlier tradition of Eurocommunism to adopt openly social democratic principles. As such, under the Blairite Massimo d'Alema the PDS entered the Olive Tree coalition government of Romano Prodi in 1996. In the wake of 1989 the Communist Party of Great Britain was renamed the Democratic Left and under the leadership of Nina Temple completed an ideological evolution that had been in the making long before the fall of communism.[40] The destruction of the party's traditional links with radical trade unionists deprived it of the social base that had made the party a force in British society for so long.

In France the long reign of the unreconstructed George Marchais over the PCF gave way to the neo-humanist approach of Robert Hue. The dictatorship of the proletariat was left far behind as Hue insisted that communists were 'not the sole proprietors of the Communist idea' and 'did not want to undertake the transformation on their own' but were committed to 'pluralism' and 'the culture of debate'. For him Communism 'was not a dogma' nor a 'project with key in hand for a new society that it would be possible one day to "decree"'.[41] There was no more talk of abolishing the market, and on this basis the PCF joined Lionel Jospin's Socialist government as junior coalition partner in May 1997. The old belief in nationalization and the virtues of state property gave way to a new emphasis on regulation through laws rather than ownership. Having lost the battle for the state, communists now adopted aspects of the liberal critique of state bureaucracy and sought to reinvigorate the tradition of self-managing socialism. The 'party organ', the newspaper *L'Humanité* founded in 1904 by Jean Jaurès, distanced itself from the Party and removed the hammer and sickle from its masthead – but its circulation continued to decline towards the 50,000 mark.

The new spirit of post-ideological politics was in evidence in India, too. An example of this was the premiership of Inder Kumar Gujral, a former communist who appointed a committed liberalizer to head the finance ministry. The Communist Party of India (Marxist-Leninist) (CPI(M)) contested the February 1998 elections as part of a united front of regional and left-wing parties and at one point was prepared to set aside ideological considerations to support its long-time rival, the Congress Party, in a bid to prevent the Hindu nationalist Bharatiya Janata Party assuming office. It might be noted that Indian democracy provides a radical exception from the 'preconditions' and 'consolidation' scenarios outlined in the stereotypical academic literature on 'democratization'. It is not only corruption and endemic rule avoidance that characterize Indian public life, but also the cross-cutting allegiances of clan, religion, ethnic group and region on which a crudely socialist-oriented state economy and political bureaucracy were superimposed that made Indian politics so exceptional. The federal system allowed a democratically elected communist government to remain in power in Kerala (a coalition of the Communist Party of India and the CPI(M)), which ran one of the more competent administrations with a developed welfare system in one of India's poorest states. Elsewhere smouldering peasant revolts in Bihar and other regions followed the example of the Maoist armed communist groups in the Naxalbari district of West Bengal. Although the latter were ruthlessly suppressed, the name 'Naxalite' lives on as a form of armed peasant struggle against landlords.

The Japanese Communist Party (JCP) became a significant opposition force as the Asian economic crisis intensified in the late 1990s and the mainstream parties appeared incapable of undertaking serious reform. In the general election of October 1996 the JCP secured 7.3 million votes (13 per cent), its best performance ever, and it strengthened its presence in municipal assemblies. The realignment of party politics of the early 1990s had seen the emergence of the New Frontier Party (NFP) to displace the ruling Liberal Democratic Party (LDP) for a time, but by 1998 the NFP had disintegrated while the Social Democratic Party, traditionally the main left alternative, had discredited itself by allying with the LDP. In broad terms it appeared that postcommunist communist parties could only survive by breaking their commitment to revolutionary socialism, but by doing so they removed their *raison d'être*. They could reprofile themselves as the radical wing of liberal democracy, but then why call themselves 'communist'?

Communism after communism

The fate of the idea of Communism became bound up with the destiny of the countries where communism was established. The defeat of Nazism and the exhaustion of communism appeared to leave no alternative ideology able to compete with the universal claims of democratic liberalism. For many, however, such a formulation is tendentious. Ligachev, for example, was clear that such a statement was malicious:

> Yeltsin's statement that Communism will not reappear in Russia, made to noisy applause in the U.S. Congress, proved false ... Can anyone bury Communism as an idea of social justice, the embodiment of the age-old dream of laboring humanity? Of course not. Communism can be eliminated only by wiping out the working people, but if that were to happen, humanity would disappear. No, it is as impossible to wipe out Communism as it is unthinkable to extinguish the sun.[42]

Communism originated in the belief that capitalism ultimately could not deliver the goods. Contrary to catastrophist expectations, capitalism proved remarkable regenerative, in particular in the post-war 'golden years' up to the mid-1970s, and for most of the developed world it demonstrated a remarkable ability to deliver rising standards of living. It was not, however, able to resolve some of the pressing problems facing humanity (cultural, environmental and inequality issues above all), and it is on this terrain that communism survives. The difficulty facing postcommunist communism, however, is that even when it might be accepted that capitalism has its limitations, there is no overwhelming reason to consider communism a viable alternative. Thus it becomes little more than a vehicle for protest, an element in the class struggle in Indian villages, the anti-corruption party in Italy, the anti-racist party in France, the party of the national idea and anti-Westernism in Russia, but of its emancipatory claims little remains.

As the memory of the communist regimes faded, nostalgia for what they appeared to represent grew – a phenomenon known as *Ostalgie* in Eastern Germany. Survey evidence suggested that the number of Czechs who said that they would prefer to live under the old regime had risen from 18 per cent in early 1997 to 29 per cent in 1998.[43] Sympathy for the past was strongest among pensioners and manual workers. Memories of controlled rents, stable prices, secure jobs, social stability were all the more attractive in conditions of inflation and rising prices for staples, rents and utilities accompanied by a perception of rising criminality and corruption. In Russia, Ukraine and other former Soviet republics this nostalgia was reflected in a strong and persistent vote for successor communist parties. The cruel notion of the 'good genocide' reflected the view that the communist vote would only decline once the old generation died out. This was an embittered generation who understood that at least a considerable part of their life had been wasted, and who felt deceived that their loyal service for so many years was now not only not respected but indeed tarnished with shades of collaboration.

Paradoxes and Paradigms

Havel noted that '[f]or long decades, the chief nightmare of the democratic world was communism. Today ... it would seem as though another nightmare has replaced it: post-communism'.[1] It is the more universal aspects of postcommunism that we will now examine. Following Hobsbawm's habit, let us dub the postcommunist epoch 'the age of paradox'. If the paradox at the heart of the communist phenomenon was how a great ideal turned into a great crime, for many postcommunism is the reverse. As Havel indicates, postcommunism was not just 'something that makes life difficult for the rest of the world' but represented 'a challenge to thought and to action'. In the second part of this chapter we will examine some of the broad theoretical paradigms of our age and their relationship to postcommunism, but first we will explore some of these paradoxes.

Paradoxes

The notion of paradox is much over-used but reflects the spirit of the modern age. In his essay, 'What is Enlightenment?', Kant was one of the first to note 'a strange and unexpected pattern in human affairs (such as we shall always find if we consider them in the widest sense), in which nearly everything is paradoxical'.[2] It is in this spirit of paradoxicality if not Enlightenment that we shall conduct our enquiry into the ambiguities of the postcommunist experience.

The anti-revolutionary revolutions

The very nature of postcommunism suggests a dualism, communism and what comes after; yet the other duality, between communism and its antithesis, anti-communism, is equally dynamic. While post-modernism is premissed on modernity but aware of its limitations, postcommunism is not the continuation of communism to its next evolutionary stage but founded on its alternative. Postcommunism is the repudiation of communism, and out of this emerges both the idea of transcendence (discussed in Chapter 2) and the dynamic of anti-revolution. These anti-revolutions were 'transcending revolutions', overcoming not only state socialist regimes in particular countries and the associated structures of the cold war, but also the very logic of Enlightenment revolutionism itself.

The events of 1989–91 were not counter-revolutionary but anti-revolutionary in two senses: they tried to overcome the actual revolutions that had taken place in these countries; and they repudiated the whole logic of revolutionary thinking that had haunted the European imagination for some two centuries. Our argument is that the end of the revolution in Russia and Eastern Europe signifies the end of Enlightenment revolutionism as a form of political action in its entirety.[3] The revolutions of 1989–91 not only challenged revolutionary theory, but also suggest that the concept of revolution itself is anachronistic. The revolutionary epoch, begun in the early modern period with the dissolution of the feudal order and monolithic religious system, reached its apogee in the eighteenth century and ended with the decline of modernity itself. The age of Enlightenment revolutionism ends with a revolution. The paradox is deliberate: the revolutions of 1989–91 were anti-revolutionary revolutions. As Andrew Arato puts it, we are confronted by 'the historical novelty of 'revolutions' that reject *the tradition* of modern revolutions'.[4]

The revolutions of 1989–91 not only put an end to a particular revolutionary cycle (namely, that begun by the Russian revolution of 1917), but also mark the conclusion of the whole era of what we shall call Enlightenment revolutionism, and indeed, to a whole epoch of how we understand politics and processes of social change.[5] Koselleck described how Enlightenment utopianism became transformed into a philosophy of history in which, in his view, the necessarily separate sphere of politics was subverted by the social, cultural and moral demands made on it. The growing gulf between state and society, politics and ethics, gave rise to the challenge in the form of what he calls *critique* (one type of which was revolutionism), and this in turn provoked a *crisis* in which the autonomy of politics and state-craft was undermined.[6] Enlightenment revolutionism assumed that complex problems of human organization could be resolved by radical intervention if those intervening had made the correct critique and borne the correct philosophy of history.[7] The revolutionary act itself was to create new political identities. The anticommunist revolutions of 1989–91 repudiated this vision of European Enlightenment revolutionism, both in content and form, and thus put an end to a whole epoch of European history. The paradox that we are suggesting here is that it took a revolution of a very specific kind, which we call an anti-revolution, to repudiate Enlightenment revolutionism, one that marks an important turning point in the trajectory of European development.

The communist revolutions were part of the triumph of modernist discourses associated with the Enlightenment project, of rational organization and progress, and thus by implication denied culture and tradition.[8] Revolutionary socialist ideology drew liberally from the Enlightenment perspective of progress, deculturation and denationalization. Condorcet's project called for 'the destruction of all historical civilizations and the standardization of mankind according to the pattern of the Paris intellectual'.[9] For Marx, too, a change of institutions was not enough but the revolutionary act itself was assumed to lead to a change of heart that would inaugurate a qualitatively new epoch. The destructive storm launched by Lenin after October 1917 failed even to reach the level of 'the Paris intellectual' but was patterned after the standards of a deracinated 'Russian' intellectual with a severe behavioural disorder. Walicki has recently demonstrated, nevertheless, how close the Bolshevik revolution remained to the basic Marxist vision, above all the destruction of commodity production and all that this entailed.[10]

The events of 1989–91 were anti-revolutions in the most profound sense. In the past those who opposed revolutions were called 'counter-revolutionaries', a term coined by Condorcet[11] and applied by the Bolsheviks to define their opponents in their own terms. The revolution was everything and everything was conducted within its frame of reference. In the French and Russian revolutions the discourse of revolution itself became one of the main forms in which the tyranny sustained itself. The insurgency of 1989–91, however, moved beyond the discourse of revolutionary thinking that kept them in thrall, and precisely in this sought freedom. To borrow Joseph de Maistre's distinction, the rejection of revolutionary socialism was not 'a *contrary revolution*' (a counter-revolution, narrowly defined), but 'the *contrary of revolution*' (opposed to the revolutionary process in its entirety).[12] The former found few takers, while the latter triumphed. The Eastern European anti-revolutions reflected the end of belief in the liberating potential of revolutionary socialism, and associated with that the end of belief in the radical emancipatory potential of the revolutionary act itself. Revolutions of the oppressed and the downcast will of course continue, but the special late eighteenth-century view of revolution as a distinctly emancipatory act casting aside the burden of superstition, obscurantism and tradition to allow access to the sunlit uplands of modernity is irrevocably dead. The Marxist accretion to the tradition of Enlightenment revolutionism that a particular class by rising up will achieve some universal goals in the development of humanity has also gone.

Those who opposed the events of 1989–91 were not labelled counter-revolutionaries because that would have legitimated their opposition and conceded precisely the intellectual terrain that the anti-revolutionists sought to free from the burden of Enlightenment revolutionism. It would have meant adopting the language of the system that they sought to transcend. The avoidance of the traditional militarized lexicon of revolutions ('liberate', 'destroy') also made obvious tactical sense, since if it came to shooting the regimes were clearly at an advantage. The exhaustion of revolutionary discourse, moreover, was apparent in the fact that very few defenders of the old regime themselves had the courage to talk in terms of defending the gains of the revolution. The order on which revolutionary socialism was based, as Horváth and Szakolczai point out, had already undergone a long process of internal dissolution even before the events of 1989–91 shouldered it aside.[13] The revolutions of 1989–91 generated a miserably weak counter-revolutionary movement for the obvious reason that the historical conjuncture that the original socialist revolutions reflected had long since disappeared. The concept of socialist revolution had itself become an irrelevance, and in the absence of a new universal transformatory ideology, the totalistic Enlightenment concept of revolution fell into decrepitude.

Postcommunism is postmodern in the paradoxical sense that it returns to pre-modern traditions truncated by the triumph of modernity from the late eighteenth century. The link forged in the furnace of the industrial revolution between social conditions and social classes and mass political action has been broken, and now once again 'postmaterialist' (or more accurately, 'pre-materialist') values come to the fore. The cultural logic of political action in new social movements from the West complements the anti-revolutionary revolutions from the East.[14] The new humanism appeals to universal values, most evident in the writings of Havel, rather than to class-based or partial values. The anti-revolutionaries of the new social movements and anti-communism appeal to the independence of civil society, the autonomy of the subject and the role of morality in politics.

The shift in the subject of the revolution is accompanied by a renewed emphasis on Tocquevillian themes, the primacy of culture over socially determined modalities of political action – and indeed, the relativization of directed political action. Contrary to Marx (in Ash's words), 'consciousness ultimately determines being ... the key to the future lies not in the external, objective condition of states – political, military, economic, technological – but in the internal subjective condition of individuals'.[15] Ethics and morality, 'living by truth' and rejecting the lie, acted as potent weapons against the party-state, although we have already expressed doubts over whether they could be equally efficacious against the tyranny of the market. Although the new culturalism has not gone unchallenged, with Skocpol insisting that 'anthropological ideas about cultural systems' are full of pitfalls in complex stratified societies,[16] the 1989–91 anti-revolutions represented a qualitative reappraisal of the scope for revolutionary political action to ameliorate the contingency of human affairs.

There is an enormous literature on revolutions, but the nature of *revolutionism* as an intellectual phenomenon and a political practice has been obscured. The fundamental paradox of the end of communist power is that a political discourse that was obsessed by the concept of revolution came to an end in a surge of revolutionary activism that itself was dedicated to putting an end not only to this specific revolution but also to the traditional practices of revolutionism in their entirety. The anti-communist revolutions of 1989–91 transcended the logic of modern vanguardist revolutions by espousing specific rather than universal goals, by transcending sectarian agendas with national ones, and by rejecting rather than innovating (although the very logic of rejection was a major innovation). If the 1980s had been characterized by the notion of 'anti-politics', whereby 'actually existing socialism' was to be transcended by indifference rather than by confrontation, then these were 'anti-revolutions', repudiating the dynamic of revolution and counter-revolution in their entirety. In short, postcommunism is post-revolutionism.

These were traditional revolutions in the sense that there was some popular mobilization based on a clear consciousness of the strength of the people as an oppressed class, and they were 'Marxist' to the extent that they took place precisely in conditions where the old regime acted as a fetter on the forces of production, where modernization had reached such a point that the old political structures had become outmoded. The subject of the anti-revolution, however, was not the proletariat but 'the people', a category that strikingly re-emerged as an autonomous actor at this time, however raw and unformed and subject to manipulation. In Marx's vision of revolution the proletariat was envisaged as the great majority of the people in revolt against the power of capital; now the people rose up to overthrow the political rule of the supposed liberators. These revolutions were directed not to fulfil the Marxist promise but to transcend it.

The anti-revolution (and everything else) 'betrayed'

The attempt to transcend the revolutionary socialist utopian project is itself a utopia and, in the manner of all systematic attempts to achieve a goal, liable to disappointment and betrayal. The transcending revolutions against communism took place on two levels: the systemic and the personal. The systemic included the elements of self-transcendence whereby old élites became part of the new ruling class, while at the personal level dissent represented a deeper popular movement of revulsion against the old regimes. The triumph of the first process could only be regarded as a betrayal by representatives of the second. Every success of postcommunism as a movement of economic transformation represented an implicit repudiation of postcommunism as an act of moral renewal. Above all, the balance between constraints and contingency changed radically: there is apparently no longer a revolutionary option to the management of political contingency, of controlling the blind forces that shape the destinies of humanity. If nothing else, this is what the *événements* of 1968 were all about.

This tragic logic is most apparent when we examine the fate of some of the figures most closely associated with the emancipatory potential of postcommunism. We have already mentioned Havel's critique of Klaus's single-minded pursuit of a neo-liberal agenda at the expense of the humanistic features he associated with civil society's potential for self-development. Solzhenitsyn had for long been the prophet of postcommunism, yet when the system that he so despised fell he appeared stranded with little to offer the post-communist world. His delay in returning until 1994 in part accounts for the erosion of his popularity, together with his surprisingly sympathetic (and probably correct) interpretation of the October 1993 events, when Yeltsin's tanks bombarded the Russian White House (the seat of the old parliament). *Événements* have now given way to mere 'events'. A series of didactic lectures on prime-time television in 1995 telling Russians how they should live, from a man who had spent 20 years in Vermont, appeared the final straw. Perhaps the most tragic figure of the postcommunist era, however, was Gorbachev, the man who had done more than any individual to make it possible. His venture into postcommunist politics in the 1996 Russian presidential elections netted him the paltry total of 386,000 votes (0.51 per cent). Neither Solzhenitsyn nor Gorbachev appeared to have anything constructive to say about the problems facing postcommunist societies or proved able to enunciate a viable alternative.

Postcommunism represented not only the repudiation of communism itself, but also of reform communism. While Dubček was venerated as the symbol of the Prague Spring, there was no effective role for him to play in the new order. More specifically, Zdeněk Mlynář, one of the leading lights of 1968 and an exponent of Gorbachevite 'modern democratic socialism', had hastened to Prague from his long exile in Vienna as communism fell, yet within a day realized that the old programme of 'socialism with a human face' had absolutely no resonance in the new circumstances. More than that, reform communists were tainted with complicity in the sins of the old regime. This was the fate of the so-called *shestdesy-atniki* (people of the 1960s) in the Soviet Union, those who espoused Khrushchev-type reformism, who thought that their time had at last come when Gorbachev launched *perestroika*, and although many played a prominent part in the changes, they soon appeared anachronistic and became marginalized as a new generation of 'democratic' politicians emerged.

The dynamic of communist dissolution suggests a failure, whereas decolonization was experienced as a great act of self-affirmation. Although for the Central and Eastern European countries the fall of communism represented liberation from the Soviet yoke, it also represented the repudiation of some of their own native socialist traditions. In Czechoslovakia, for instance, the strong inter-war labour movement in the immediate post-war years gave the communists a solid basis of support, while the experience of 'socialism with a human face' in 1968 sought to affirm both an indigenous and universal affirmation of humanistic socialist values. In Poland Solidarity reflected a long and deep tradition of aspirations of worker self-management. These traditions, as well as communism itself, were repudiated by the postcommunist transitions.

Opinion polls in the late communist years suggested widespread public support for the market and competition, but there were widely different interpretations of what exactly they implied.[17] The market tended to be represented as something benignly abstract with little understanding of the often malicious character of market *forces*. The most obvious paradox is that liberal leaders who distrusted planning and who claimed to reassert the autonomy of the market were forced by the logic of the transition itself to manage the transformation process with as much authority as any central planner of old. This tension is particularly stark with respect to Klaus, who frequently condemned social planning and emphasized the unpredictable and spontaneous nature of reform,[18] yet as prime minister of the Czech Republic from 1991 to 1997 ruled with a heavy-handed interventionism. The rapid conversion of those who in the 1980s espoused Solidarity's programme for a 'self-managing republic' and an extended welfare state to support for extreme economic liberalism in 1989 has often been commented on.[19]

While the Solidarity government might have come to power and then proceeded to repudiate almost all the principles for which it had fought, few accuse the Mazowiecki government of 'betrayal'. At a deeper level the government in launching shock therapy was fulfilling the underlying aims of the movement, namely the achievement of a rational economy. Similarly, the Yeltsin regime fulfilled certain of the tasks of the insurgent democratic movement. Paradoxically, the revolution could only be fulfilled by being betrayed – and thus it always was with revolutions. The notion of betrayal itself here has to be understood as part of the very logic of revolution.

The transformative process itself becomes the key characteristic of these polities, although transformation in and of itself tells us little about the dynamic of politics. The view that the democratic revolution was betrayed, or at least hijacked, is prevalent in postcommunist countries and accounts for much of the sense of popular disappointment, yet is based on a misrepresentation of historical processes that assumes that idealism can somehow be subsumed into the organization of human affairs. This is not to suggest that a cynical 'realist' view of human affairs is the only appropriate one, but merely to argue that revolutions have their own logic that, while amenable to emancipatory popular interventions, must at least be understood before cries of 'betrayal' are uttered.

The postcommunist 'betrayal' was not restricted to the former communist countries. For Günter Grass the unification of Germany was an unmitigated disaster for both parties to the 'union'. Despite joining together in one state, the two 'nations' resolutely moved away from each other. For Grass, unification represented the destruction of all that the Federal Republic had stood for: 'Without communist prompting, the class society which we once believed we had overcome through "social democracy" has reconstituted itself'.[20] The balance between capital and labour had been disrupted and the opportunities for social renewal offered by unification squandered. The paradox here is that at precisely the moment when diversity became possible, the variety in social forms – both within societies and between different types of societies – was severely reduced. Togliatti's, and indeed de Gaulle's, vision of a pluralist, multipolar and diverse Europe has disappeared.

For other countries the betrayal is more than simply disappointment at the reality of postcommunism but of the very lifeblood of victory in war, of which communism was only a part. China's liberation from Japanese invasion and a century of humiliation at the hands of the West, Russia's (and Ukraine's, and Belorussia's, . . . – why does such a list add up to less than 'the USSR's'?) victory over Nazi Germany, and Vietnam's triumph in the twentieth century's longest war in which 3 million died and 300,000 are still missing, of these only China's victory has not yet been vitiated. In Vietnam the dollar has effectively take over from the dong, giving America control over fiscal policy. In the postscript to his *Vietnam: Anatomy of a War*, Gabriel Kolko wrote that the war finally ended in 'the defeat of all who fought in it – and one of the great tragedies of modern history'.[21] He condemned the Communist Party's embrace of the market after 1986 and its capitulation in the face of 'globalization', above all the destruction of a relatively egalitarian society and the erosion of welfare services.[22]

'Political' economy and 'economical' politics

Sassoon nicely captures the irony of revisionism (and by extension, of postcommunism, too): 'The paradox of the new revisionists was that while they were relinquishing belief in the "continuous upward line of social progress", they were adopting a belief in the "continuous upward line" of economic growth under capitalism'.[23] Postcommunism involves a distinctive relationship between politics and economics. According to Malia, 'once the Party had been disestablished, the relationship of political to economic change was reversed. In the postcommunist situation it is the process of economic reform that governs the prospect for democracy'.[24] Antirevolutions that sought to wrest politics from its alleged subordination to the 'objective' laws of history found themselves tightly bound to the logic of economic transformation. In the initial stages of these new great transformations politics remained in command as the state divested itself of direct control over economic life through privatization and the like. In some countries strong governments remained in control to oversee the process of economic liberalization, but the logic of state action here was functional rather than ideological. Even moderate forms of statism appeared to be delegitimated. Economic policy was repoliticized at the very time that postcommunists everywhere proclaimed the need to allow the market free rein. At the same time, politics itself was 'economized' because of the weakness of the state and the interpenetration of political and economic interests in the postcommunist world.

While postcommunism intersects with the notion of post-industrial society, the latter is far from being a post-economic society. Bell summarized his understanding of the former as follows:

> Broadly speaking, if industrial society is based on machine technology, post-industrial society is shaped by an intellectual technology. And if capital and labor are the major structural features of industrial society, information and knowledge are those of the post-industrial society.[25]

The paradox here is that, contrary to Bell, the modern age is dominated and penetrated to an ever greater extent by capital repro-
duction strategies, not only at the level of the enterprise but also by
the state in the global system and the individual in local society. The
market has now attained the status of part of the natural order of
things. Resistance to its penetration into every sphere of social life,
including organized religion and academia, has all but crumbled
into passive and futile grumbles in vestries and senior common
rooms.

While postcommunism represents the economization of politics,
the focus of analysis has shifted away from what Marxists used to
call 'the forces of production' and its associated social relations
towards constitutive approaches that focus on the political and
cultural dimensions of modern societies and questions of 'identity'
and self-fulfilment. At precisely the moment when political
economy approaches (of which Marxism is only one) to the
problem of the vastly extended invasive properties of contemporary capitalism into daily life and social relations might have shed
some light on the problem (if not offer any solutions), these
approaches are labelled 'economistic' or 'reductionist' and dis-
carded in favour of culturalist interpretations of the postmodern
sort.

The global antagonism between communism and capitalism represented the confrontation between two logics of the rationalism of
modernity.[26] The conflict stabilized a distinctive model of rational
modernity, and with its passing both entered a period of crisis. The
existence of two competing systems, formalized in the conventions
of the cold war after 1945, forced capitalism itself to adjust and
reform. While it would certainly be an exaggeration to argue that
modern welfare states were born as a result of the cold war, in the
advanced societies the existence of an alternative often prompted
concessions to the demands of the labour movement. Paradoxically,
the communist challenge helped capitalist societies become more
just and, by broadening the basis of national consensus and the
depth of the national market, more effective. This external corrective has now disappeared.

The malicious dialectic between triumph and defeat is visible in
yet another sphere. The triumph of neo-liberalism over communism may well lead to the diminution of the West's influence over the
rest of the world, having lost the comparative advantage of a

'better' economic system. The fall of communism deprived capitalism not only of its rival but, in a paradoxical way, also of an inept
competitor that served to highlight capitalism's advantages. The
removal of communism has accentuated the weaknesses of capitalism and the shortcomings of neo-classical economic theory. Stiglitz
recently argued that the neo-classical model fails to take into
account the problems arising from the lack of information and the
costs of acquiring information, and also from the imperfections in
some markets.[27] In a more dramatic vein, Thurow has argued that
if no remedial measures are taken then capitalism will not so much
collapse as stagnate.[28] More specifically, in the USA the adaptation
to the postcommunist economy is accompanied by increased
exploitation and labour insecurity to compensate, some would
argue, for the drop in profits gained from conducting the cold war.

This brings us to perhaps the ultimate paradox of the fall of
communism, one identified by the pre-Marxist Adam Müller
(1779–1829). He argued that the market would be unable to establish a stable equilibrium between supply and demand. According to
James D. White, he was 'the first to suggest that capitalism was a
self-contradictory system, which, if allowed to develop to its logical
conclusion, to the formation of a world market, would undermine
its own foundations and bring about its own destruction'.[29] Postcommunism has ushered in the epoch of a world market with a
vengeance, but lacking either a polar opposite against which to
develop or an effective critique from within, may find that its
pathologies, held in check by the revolutionary challenge, may now
flourish freely. The ultimate paradox may be that capitalism needed
communism, its alter ego, to sustain its own viability. Marx may well
be proved right in the end, but the prospect of an age that is both
postcommunist and post-capitalist reaches for the other shore of
the imagination.

We will now turn to paradigms.

Paradigms

The end of the communist era entailed theoretical shifts affecting
not only the former communist countries but also the wider
world. Although Habermas argued that not a single theoretical
innovation came out of Eastern Europe,[30] while Offe stressed the

untheoretical nature of these revolutions, and in his last book the historian of the French revolution, François Furet, asserted that 'nothing else is visible in the ruins of the communist societies other than the familiar repertoire of liberal democracy',[31] they missed the larger significance of the onset of postcommunism. The final phase of the transcendence of communism brought into play a rich tradition that was anything but untheoretical or bereft of ideas in character, in particular the logic of the 'anti-revolution'. The fall of communism, moreover, was accompanied by the assertion of a number of paradigms that sought to give shape to the significance of the event.

The end of communism . . . and of history?

There is a broad consensus that the communist experiment failed, but there is far less agreement over the philosophical significance of the end of communism. Krishan Kumar notes that '1989 spelled the end of several major projects in modern European history'.[32] Revolutionary socialism was undoubtedly one of the great projects of modernity, with its roots in the Enlightenment belief in the perfectibility of human affairs through reason and rational organization, and became one of the major 'metanarratives' of the twentieth century. Its alleged demise is associated not just with the end of utopianism itself, but with the very ideal of human emancipation and societal self-fulfilment.

Francis Fukuyama went further, announcing contentiously that we are witnessing 'the end of history': 'that is, the end point of mankind's ideological evolution and the universalisation of Western liberal democracy as the final form of human government . . . the unabashed victory of economic and political liberalism'.[33] Fukuyama argues that communism and fascism were simply detours and regressions in the development of liberal democracy over the last two centuries. Communism failed because it was not a genuine alternative but a symptom of the growing pains of global liberal society. Its failure was inevitable, given the certainty of liberalism's triumph. Despite Fukuyama's conviction about the ultimate triumph of liberalism, he does not argue that we are experiencing the end of history as it is commonly understood. He does not deny the great potential of nationalism, racism, feminism and environmental degradation, or the powerful challenge from various forms of fundamentalism, to alter the course of history.

> To refute my hypothesis it is not sufficient to suggest that the future holds in store large and momentous events. One would have to show that these events were driven by a systematic idea of political and social justice that claimed to supersede liberalism.[34]

The end of history as ideology, according to Fukuyama, does not mean the end of conflict, but that any conflicts that do arise are not global but emerge out of local outbreaks of religious fundamentalism, of nationalism, of national marginalization or humiliation. 'Are there, in other words,' Fukuyama asks, 'any fundamental "contradictions" in human life that cannot be resolved in the context of modern liberalism, that would be resolved by an alternative political-economic structure?'[35]

Fukuyama's analysis represents an inverted form of Marxist historicism, the application of historical materialism to serve opposed ends. For Marx the end of history was the end of capitalist exploitation. After 1917 the Soviet system was isolated, and thus could claim that history would only end when communism became a universal system: history had to be abolished everywhere or it could not be abolished anywhere. Marxist historicism comes up against Fukuyama's liberal historicism, a phenomenon that to most liberals is a contradiction in terms. Liberals have big ideas about liberty and the role of the individual, but do not usually (unless they are Whigs) have much to say about history. It is for this reason that traditional liberals (like Dahrendorf) found Fukuyama's ideas repugnant.

Fukuyama's historicism generalizes from the broad sweep of contemporary history to provide an all-encompassing key to social evolution, but (like Marx's earlier) ultimately remains unconvincing. History is by definition dynamic and is characterized by the unexpected, although not necessarily the contingent. The demise of the most sustained challenge to liberal democracy with the fall of the communist states in 1989–91 does not necessarily entail liberalism's inevitable triumph. It would be a mistake to assume that capitalism is inherently democratic; this was certainly not the case in the interwar years, and although since 1945 there is much evidence to suggest that liberal democracy is the 'best possible shell' for the development of global capitalism, the relationship between the two remains problematical. While liberal democracy and capitalism might be inseparable, the establishment of the latter does not necessarily signal the triumph of the former. The liberalization of the former communist economies has enormously expanded opportunites, but also marked the onset of 'hustler capitalism'. On the international level, globalization means the intensification of the marketization of human life, the dissolution of the very concept of exploitation, the marginalization of whole social groups (and indeed some countries) and the erosion of the ability of the state and social movements to intervene in defence of 'traditional' social values, but opened up new areas of contestation and generalized crisis.

From ideology to culture

As so often in the past, Samuel Huntington laid the foundations for a paradigm shift in the appreciation of the nature of international relations in the postcommunist order. His study of *The Clash of Civilizations*, predicting 'tribal conflict on a global scale', adopted a Spenglerian tone about the decline of America from the perspective of the comparative study of the rise and fall of civilizations: 'The West's victory in the Cold War has produced not triumph but exhaustion'. With the disappearance of the USSR, the West lacks (in Stephen Holmes's words) 'a sustaining and ennobling enmity',[36] provoking a global identity crisis. With the demise of one enemy, Huntington seeks to resurrect a new one. The age of ideological conflict gives way to 'an era dominated by ethnic conflict and fault-line wars between groups from different civilizations'. With the collapse of communism, 'culture replaced ideology as the magnet of attraction and repulsion'. A mature civilization like that of the West is susceptible to the challenge of the 'surging civilizations' of the Chinese or Islamic types.[37] Huntington noted that:

> The West is and will remain for years to come the most powerful civilisation. Yet its power relative to other civilizations is declining ... A central axis of post cold war politics is the interaction of western power and culture with the power and culture of non-western civilizations.[38]

Civilizations like the Chinese have pursued modernization while rejecting Westernization, and the Japanese have been able to 'adapt western techniques to the Japanese spirit', as the Japanese reformers put it.

A cultural relativism pervades the work that underestimates the vitality of the liberal universalism that has become the corner-stone of the declarations of multilateral organizations in the post-war era. From the Universal Declaration of Human Rights in 1948 to the Helsinki Final Act, universal liberal principles were enshrined as the basis of whatever there was of the common world order. Not internationalism as such, but a broader and more inclusive universalism lies at the basis of postcommunism. Huntington, moreover, fails to take into account the multiplicity of identities people have in modern cosmopolitan states. Cultural traditions are far from monolithic, and indeed are increasingly displaced by the synthetic world 'civilization' of modernity. Giddens uses the term 'post-traditional' not to suggest that tradition has disappeared but that it has lost its privileged status in society. Rather than one's social identity being determined by birth and place, it is in a constant process of 'construction' through choices and decisions. The language of 'fundamentalism', whether based on the Koran or the Bible, is a response by cultures challenged by the homogenizing principles of Westernization ('a banner of their despair and a weapon of their rage', as Manuel Castells put it[39]) but it is also about the profound inequities structured into the international system since the end of the cold war. As Graham Fuller argues,

> 'Civilizational clash' is not so much over Jesus Christ, Confucius or the Prophet Muhammed as it is over the unequal distribution of world power, wealth, and influence, and the perceived historical lack of respect accorded to small states and peoples by larger ones. Culture is the vehicle for expression of conflict, not its cause.[40]

The disadvantaged world is not alone in engaging in 'culture wars'; in the United States conservatives, having lost their communist protagonist, have turned inwards to attack 'alternative lifestyles', abortion, Darwinism and the intelligence of certain races, and lost the intellectual edge that once characterized their thinking.[41]

The challenge of democratization cannot be spirited away through culturalist formulations. While Huntington is right to argue that 'much of the world is becoming more modern and less western',[42] accompanied by the denunciation of 'human rights imperialism', it is too easy for authoritarian regimes to gainsay the extension of civil, human and national rights as somehow alien to their native traditions. This is not to advocate the undifferentiated and monolithic assertion of Western values, but to suggest that these values can no longer (if they ever were) be considered solely Western. Since at least the Second World War and the adoption of landmark documents such as the Universal Declaration of Human Rights, framed in part by the Soviet Union and to which most members of the United Nations have given their uncoerced assent, human rights have become the concern of the international community at large and not just of the West. There is a third category between Westernization and modernization that we call 'universalization', the combination of universal human rights concerns with respect for indigenous traditions and practices. It is the balance between the two that is the issue, not the wholesale adoption or rejection of one or the other.

While Huntington deals with the culturation of politics at the global level, there is a vigorous tradition (of which Eurocommunism was an important strand) that reinterpreted the way organizations and polities function and change in cultural terms. In Britain, for example, Stuart Hall argued:

> Culture has transformed our conception of power, which we used to think of in a rather crude and reductionist way. Instead of seeing power simply in terms of government or the military, it is everywhere, from the family and gender relations to sport and personal relationships. Our very identities and subjectivities are formed culturally.[43]

This is no doubt the case, but if politics is everywhere, by the same token it is nowhere: traditional organizations like trade unions and even political parties are dissolving into a new world of image-makers, quangos, lobbyists, 'partnerships' dominated by business leaders spurning the expertise of educational and other professionals, and virtual global politics. The election of New Labour under Tony Blair on 1 May 1997 represented a cultural shift of momentous import, but the renewed 'project' of modernizing Britain could only be sustained by subjecting itself to critique. The language of that critique, and thus sources of renewal of the project itself, remain unclear.

Capitalism after communism

The Soviet past, now painted in uniformly black colours, appears to stand as a testimony to the evil that emerges out of misdirected social idealism. Yet the perceived need to establish some ethical constraints on capitalism, and indeed, to counter the potentially catastrophic consequences of unfettered global markets, has been recognized even by some of the leading capitalists, notably the speculator and philanthropist George Soros.[44] Soros observed: 'Although I have made a fortune in the financial markets I now fear that the untrammeled [*sic*] intensification of *laissez-faire* capitalism and the spread of market values into all areas of life is endangering our open and democratic society'.[45] He warned that global financial markets were not self-regulating, but it was not clear how free-market fundamentalism could be reined in. As Will Hutton puts it: 'The world's financial markets need to be brought to heel. They themselves do not spontaneously provide international order; it has to be created by public agency and then governed, which means rule by some supra-national authority.'[46] How this 'authority' is to be constituted and who would control it remains unclear, but it is the diagnosis rather than the prescription that concerns us here. Although capitalist democracies appeared to suffer from a 'legitimation crisis' in the 1970s,[47] the collapse of communism has provoked a new type of legitimacy crisis – and like all crises it may signal the beginning of healing or augur a more terminal anguish.

While the historic struggle between the marketless collectivized economy and free-market capitalism may be over, criticism of capitalism itself is by no means transcended, and indeed may be intensified since its alternative has dissolved. Socialists and old-fashioned conservatives always understood that there is a barbarism lurking at the heart of untrammelled capitalism, relentlessly subverting tradition, culture and values unless checks and balances are imposed. As the writer Lewis Lapham put it:

> The collapse of Communism at the end of the cold war removed from the world's political theatre the last pretence of a principled opposition to the rule of money, and the pages of history suggest that oligarchy unhindered by conscience or common sense seldom takes much of an interest in the cause of civil liberty.[48]

André Gorz had already argued that the free market subverts the integrity of the life-world upon which the the capitalist economy rests.[49]

Postcommunism was accompanied by the triumph of neo-liberalism and coincided with the rise of the globalization paradigm. The

International Monetary Fund (IMF) was one of the most influential institutions established by the Bretton Woods conference in
1944 to manage fixed exchange rates, but with the shift towards
ever-freer private sector capital markets after the USA left the gold
standard and devalued in 1971 it appeared that it had become
redundant. The Mexican crisis of 1982 restored the IMF as lender
of last resort to indebted developing countries, and then with the
fall of communism it became the main policeman in the implementation of the 'Washington consensus' policy prescriptions based on
fiscal austerity and economic liberalization. The IMF's headquar-
ters staff in Washington doubled and its agents roamed the postcommunist world, and then with onset of the Asian financial crisis
from late 1997 it stepped in with tailored packages for Thailand,
Indonesia and South Korea. The IMF insisted that the absence of
some sort of coordinating body exacerbated the Great Depression
from 1929, but its critics questioned whether the same prescriptions
were equally valid for all countries. Neo-liberals assume that one
coat fits all cases, whereas others insisted that the cloth needed to
be cut according to circumstances.

   In its standard form globalization suggests that '[t]he world is
embarked on a progressive emancipation from land as a determi-
nant of production and power'.[50] The end of capital controls in the
early 1970s allowed the foreign exchange market to grow 14-fold,
and today commodity trade represents only 5 per cent of global
money circulation. Economic forces emerge as an extraterritorial
power that allegedly hollows out the powers of the state and with
it the context for democratic politics: 'Domestic political change
does not suffice because it has insufficient jurisdiction to deal with
global problems. The people in a particular state cannot determine
international outcomes by holding an election.'[51] According to
Greider, governments are reduced to supplicants begging for
investment and other favours from multinational companies.[52] 'The
state will become just one of many players in the international
marketplace and will have to negotiate directly with foreign factors
of production to solve domestic economic problems.'[53] With the
ever-greater pressure to attract foreign investment, countries have
to conform to certain internationally derived norms, such as low
inflation, a stable currency, a trained and flexible labour force
and rising productivity, that may well conflict with domestic pressures for greater employment, social security and other politically

derived demands. The solution to an ever-increasing range of domestic problems can no longer be resolved by domestic politics alone. In short, globalization suggests the autonomization of social processes, a recognition that there are some things beyond the scope of conscious state intervention and regulation. Put crudely, the dominance of capital over labour takes on global and less accountable forms. Even worse, according to Viviane Forrester, labour itself has become increasingly irrelevant: workers are no longer needed by the capitalist economy. As she puts it: 'We are discovering that there is something worse than being exploited: it is to be deemed unexploitable'.[54]

Hirst and Thompson take a sceptical view: 'globalisation as conceived by the more extreme globalisers is largely a myth . . . In some respects the current international economy is less open and integrated than the regime that prevailed from 1870 to 1914'.[55] The globalization process, it has been argued by Roderick Martin in the Eastern European context, 'is countered by a contrary process of fragmentation and localisation'.[56] For Martin, globalization as such has only limited relevance for understanding postcommunist developments; rather, 'the interaction between multinational strategies and local institutional structures' is the key.[57] The economic effects of globalization may well have been exaggerated, since most of the core economic policy functions of national governments survive intact, and, indeed, the challenges of globalization are largely mediated through the national state. Just as in the latter part of the nineteenth century, when the world economy was dominated by a free trade regime, the essential dynamic is between international economic integration and sovereign nation-states. In postcommunist societies there is a renewed interest in what are called 'national development policies' reminiscent of Friedrich List's call for the protection of infant industries in 1830s Germany which focused not on trade but on investment.[58] The developmental functions of the state, pursued so effectively by Japan and South Korea earlier, were once again emphasized, for example, by Yevgenii Primakov's government in Russia.

Globalization appeared to be a euphemism for a new era of corporate rule in which the managerial class identified by Milovan Djilas and James Burnham appeared to be shaking off democratic constraints. While free trade and open capital markets are the dominant ideas of our times, an 'accountability gap' has opened up.

The liberalism that was successful in reducing the state's power, 'has created a formidable anonymous new power'.[59] The domination of the real economy by money markets was predicted by Marx, and today, according to Hoffmann, '[t]he global economy is literally out of control, not subject to the rules of accountability and principles of legitimacy that apply to relations between individuals and states'.[60] Much postcommunist thinking has criticized the idea 'that we can somehow have globalisation of opportunity without globalisation of responsibility'.[61] Just as national opportunity was followed by national accountability, so, too, global opportunity might be followed by the globalization of responsibility, above all through the principles of universalism suggested earlier where supranational agencies will have a critical role to play. For some the response is the strengthening of European federalism,[62] while others sought to rehabilitate a role for the state. Robert Reich, Clinton's labour secretary in 1993–97, advanced the formidably sounding 'post neo-classical endogenous growth theory', arguing that a country could raise its own growth rate (endogenously) by investing in human capital, above all education and training,[63] an idea taken up by New Labour.

Socialism after communism – paradigm regained?

The transcendence of communism appeared to represent the transcendence of socialism as well, although by a different route. There are no countries left pursuing a non-capitalist path of development, while everywhere non-market socialism as an instrument of modernization has been rejected. Arthur Lipow notes that 'the twentieth century has been the graveyard of ideas and movements born in the Enlightenment and given their most profound expression in the democratic labour and socialist movements'. For him, the failure of socialism was civilisation's loss as well, 'leading capitalism into a new kind of barbarism'.[64] But is the cause of some sort of 'social-ism' (as Blair once put it) entirely lost? Does the collapse of communism drag socialism down in its wake? For radical socialists such as Lipow there is little cause for cheer, while for Halliday, '[t]he Cold War, in its broader historical sense, is continuing, but with the collapse of one of the two protagonists'.[65]

Postcommunism is to a large extent post-socialism, too. McRae argues:

> It is not just that communism has collapsed; it is the whole concept of
> the command economy. The idea that countries can improve their
> economic performance by heavy state regulation of economic life is
> dead. Whereas in 1979 perhaps 40 per cent of the world's population
> lived in countries in which the market economy was the dominant
> ideology, more than 90 per cent does today.[66]

Thus, according to Skidelsky, the twentieth century and the communist challenge can be characterized as the rise and fall of collectivism.[67] The period between 1920 and 1980 was identified by Paul
Johnson as the 'collectivist era', whereas the 1990s saw the reasser-
tion of a liberal individualist hegemony. Keynesianism, the welfare
state, *dirigiste* planning and even social democracy have been sup-
planted as the *idée force* of the era by economic liberalism. Economic efficiency and market rationality have replaced notions of
social justice and equality as the towering pillars of our age. It is
now clear that the epoch's great collectivist ideologies represented
a transitory stage and we are now entering a new age of individualism, if not liberalism. It is not simply that collectivism is giving way
to a renewed impulse to individualism, since East Asian societies
and some others clearly remain intensely collectivist, but that the
logic of non-market economic collectivism has been undermined.

Marx might have been thrown off his pedestal, but the Keynesian demand management model of the economy has also been
challenged.[68] Keynesianism overestimated the government's ability
to manage the economy through the manipulation of macroeconomic fiscal instruments to stabilize the economy and reduce
unemployment. Economic neo-liberalism in the 1980s challenged
the very premises of this sort of state interventionism to correct
the inadequacies of the market in the business cycle. Above all, the
seemingly inexorable rise of the share of public spending as a pro-
portion of gross domestic product in the Western welfare states
(averaging 48 per cent in the EU today and just below 40 per cent
in Britain, but recall the dramatic fall in Russia and elsewhere, mentioned in Chapter 4) was held responsible for eroding individual
initiative and rendering industry uncompetitive by burdening it
with exorbitant non-wage costs. James Buchanan and other public
choice theorists undermined the benign view of government that
lay at the heart of Keynesianism by asserting that states, agencies,
politicians and key electorates conspire to pursue sectoral interests
at the expense of effective economic management, while Milton

Friedman (echoing comments on the fall of communism) asserted that Keynesianism was a 'failed experiment'. The old model of a centralized economy has given way to profound shifts provoked, on the one hand, by the globalization of the international economy, and, on the other, by the extension of the market principle in national economies. At the very moment when politics is being 'reborn' in postcommunist societies, the scope for politics itself is being radically undermined.

The trajectory of Western European socialism was bound up with the fate of Soviet communism, and even today the Western left has become 'conservative' in the sense that it seeks to preserve the social policy achievements of the past, and communism in the former communist states is essentially a backward-looking movement when it is communist, and when it looks forward its agenda is largely nationalistic. Innovation in the 1980s appeared to come from the right, and in the 1990s from the centre. According to Sassoon, European socialism had long been in crisis and had been unable to fulfil its primary task, the creation of a new society that was qualitatively different from capitalist society. It had, however, influenced the development of Western European societies, above all through the creation of the welfare state.[69] Willie Thompson examined the main tendencies of the left and concluded that by the end of the century they had all become exhausted or been defeated, although he, too, notes the way that for most of the last hundred years the left had set the agenda and the right had been marginalized.[70] With the collapse of inspirational ideas of progress the left, too, withered away. Capitalism could not cope with the problems of modernity, while postmodernism offered no universal solutions but only the possibility for the liberation of separate groups. The task now was to find some 'new project'.[71] The problem, according to Sassoon, was that the left had always found itself in a bind: torn between the opposing desires to improve capitalism and to destroy it, but unable to escape the fact that the very achievements of socialism were dependent on capitalism's success – wherever capitalism was in crisis, so was socialism.

The social base of classical socialist movements has been transformed at the same time as the last vestiges of a belief in the universal emancipatory role of the working class has evaporated. If socialism seeks to renew itself, it will have to find a new vehicle for change. Freed from the burden of utopia, socialism at the same time

lost its power to offer a convincing alternative and found itself confused, disheartened and marginalized. Throughout the cold war
years the repressive character of the Soviet regime, at home and
abroad (particularly the invasions of Hungary and Czechoslovakia), was thrown in the face of left radicalism as a standing and
self-defining reproach. Freed at last from this incubus, however,
instead of thriving the transformatory left has withered away. Even
relatively moderate forms of social activism have been delegit-
imized. The very terms 'left' and 'right', derived from the seating
plan of Louis XVI's États Généraux, appeared as redundant as the
slogans of the French revolution themselves: liberty might well be
a fine principle, but who needs equality and fraternity?

This does not mean that the left has disappeared entirely. Bobbio
has forcefully argued that the concept of the 'left' is drawn from the
fundamentally dyadic structure of politics and now represents the
principle of equality, and while the failure of the Eastern European
communist regimes and the dominance of the 'liberal' trend in
Europe may well have provoked a crisis within the left, the fundamental distinction between left and right has not been erased.[72]
According to public choice theorists, however, the left, through its
support for welfare agencies and active state intervention, is itself
responsible for new forms of inequality. In the postcommunist
world, moreover, the left appeared to be the vehicle for a new form
of social authoritarianism while failing to challenge the accumulat-
ing sovereignty of transnational corporations. This is not the place
to discuss the growing inequalities in neo-liberal societies, the marginalization of whole social groups, the return of Victorian diseases,
the debt burden and deteriorating terms of trade for most 'Third
World' countries, let alone what might be identified as the systemic
problems of global capitalism, but only to note that these (and
much more) may reinvigorate a postcommunist left.

The collapse of communism removed the traditional fear of the
left and opened its way to power in Italy and elsewhere. The former
socialist prime minister of France, Michel Rocard, called himself a
'free-market socialist', the former socialist prime minister of Spain,
Felipe González, spoke of 'supply-side socialism', while the Labour
Party under Blair adopted a radical modernizing agenda based on
constitutional reform and the combination of the power of the
market with a vision of social justice. The election of New Labour
in May 1997 signalled the beginning of a new era of deregulatory

society-centred socialism. The great leftist parties on the continent
remained much more traditional: Franz Vranitsky's Socialist Party
of Austria, Lionel Jospin's Socialist Party in France, Felipe
González's Socialist Workers' Party, and even Oskar Lafontaine's
SPD. The SPD's victorious candidate for the Chancellorship in the
September 1998 elections, Gerhard Schröder, used Blairite slogans
like 'the new centre', 'social responsibility' and 'modernity' but in
his home state of Lower Saxony acted as an old-fashioned interventionist German Social Democrat. To 'govern from the left' from
the late 1990s meant imposing fiscal rectitude and managing capitalist societies more effectively than capitalist parties themselves.[73]
The more intelligent sections of the old governing élites realized
this and came to support the modernizing agendas of these postcommunist socialist parties.

The intellectual charge represented by the left is by no means
over. The fall of the USSR appeared to some to suggest that the
whole field of intellectual history was outdated and representative
of an older – and redundant – mentality and could be replaced by
analysis of the development of society itself (something post-
modernist thinking is particularly prone to do). Western socialist
theory has always been one of the richest strands in intellectual
history, and in a recent defence of the discipline, drawing particularly on the experience of critical theory, Martin Jay has vigorously
reasserted the importance of ideas.[74] For others 1989–91 signals the
emancipation of socialism from false deterministic assumptions and
doomed loyalties to the Soviet 'socialist motherland', and thus at
the very least presents the potential for a progressive alternative
project to capitalism, the attempt, in E.P. Thompson's words, 'to
rediscover some vocabulary of rationality and of rehabilitated uni-
versals'.[75] Thus the collapse of state socialism presents new opportunities for the critique of capitalism. The regimes failed to deliver
the ideals of human emancipation that they promised. But what are
the bases and prospects for an ethical humanistic socialism?
Thompson insisted: 'We cannot know what spaces the third way
might inherit, after the collapse of the Cold War, unless we press in
practice beyond the old "two camps" thinking and find out'.[76] For
him the core would remain a critique of the inequalities of capitalism, a programme based on social justice, gender equality in word
and practice, anti-racism, and much else besides, including a role
for a benign interventionist state, but not nationalization, central

planning and old-style corporatist interventionism. The development of new 'socialist' government responding to these issues was made more rather than less likely as a result of the fall of the communist systems.

For revolutionary socialists the collapse of the Soviet Union represented not the failure of revolutionary socialism in its entirety but only a degenerate Stalinist version of it.[77] From this perspective Soviet socialism was 'a grotesque distortion of the communism of Marx and Engels and a betrayal of the socialist tradition from which Marxism sprang'.[78] Freed of the Stalinist incubus, this view suggests that Marxism can now resume unfinished business.[79] This entailed above all challenging the hegemony of capital, something done with great sophistication by Istvan Mészáros in his *Beyond Capital*.[80] Ellen Meiksins Wood has argued that the collapse of communism made the Marxist critique of capitalism even more relevant. Her capitalism is firmly located within the context of historical materialism, as a system of exploitative social relations and political power.[81] From this perspective revolutionary socialism failed in its first major practical attempt at implementation for a variety of conjunctural reasons (Russia's alleged backwardness, the political culture of the people and so on) but by no means represented a philosophical failure. Trotskyists would subscribe to this view, and indeed there is a solid historical pedigree to this approach. The peculiarly dogmatic version developed in the USSR by no means exhausted the varieties of anti-Leninist revolutionary socialism. Revolutionary socialism can be seen to have suffered from a progressive narrowing, from Marx through to Bolshevism, Leninism and on to Stalinism, and now the task can be seen as reversing the logic of closure and returning the tradition to its radical emancipatory roots.

A more convincing approach, however, is to accept that the failure of historical communism is not something extrinsic to the socialist problematic but an event that should be used to understand the challenges facing the theory and practice of radical socialism. For Habermas the rejection of capitalism does not mean the abolition of the market but that socialism (what he terms 'radical reformism') needs to find a way of restraining the destructive power of capitalism.[82] The anti-revolutionary repudiation of revolution as the supreme emancipatory act, in and of itself able to resolve fundamental social contradictions after which only the details have to be filled in, is accepted. The emphasis (reminiscent of Bernstein's arguments earlier) is now on process and the long-term restructuring of human relations, and thus revolutionary socialism gives way to radical socialism. As far as this view is concerned, the failure of actually existing socialism, philosophically speaking, says nothing about the possibility of establishing a genuine form of socialism. Goran Therborn, for example, argues that the crisis is unrelated to either failure or success but 'simply arose from a new historical situation to which it is simply irrelevant'.[83] There is, though, a philosophical problem. Therborn's argument that the current crisis of socialism might actually be due to its success rather than to its failure, having 'grasped and solved' a number of problems and thus in the new historical situation having little left to do, might well be valid in practical terms but leaves a gaping hole in socialist theory. Revolutionary socialism was always a future-oriented ideology, leading the way to the transcendence of class conflict and the abolition of the state, moving from the lower stage of socialism to the higher stage of communism. Without the perspective of a communist future, the bottom falls out of the philosophical basis of current revolutionary and even radical socialist politics. It is not enough to suggest that this is due to a crisis of modernity, as Therborn does, since this only reinforces the view that Marxist revolutionary socialism had always misunderstood the nature of the emergent forms of modernity.

Socialism was forced to reinvent itself in response to the needs of a postcommunist world, and this it began to do, but what remained of classical notions of socialism remained unclear. As Pierson notes of revived ideas for market socialism: 'What makes market socialism seem feasible is its attachment to the *market*, but that which makes it *socialist* is the very thing that renders it infeasible'.[84] In late nineteenth-century Britain socialism evolved out of radicalism; in the late twentieth century the movement was reversed and a revived post-socialist radicalism emerged. This included a renewed belief in the efficacy of government intervention, no longer in the form of nationalization and direct state control, but in the form of the enabling and regulatory state. The old collectivism has given way to a more focused 'clever state' based on 'realistic radicalism'. The old social democratic belief that political democracy must be accompanied by social rights is now balanced by the liberal view that individual choice and economic initiative lie at the basis of a successful society.[85] One of the leading exponents of this approach is the *Washington Post* columnist, E.J. Dionne. He insisted that 'progressives' retained a belief in the state's ability to rectify problems that the free market could not, but that the belief in active government was accompanied by a recognition of the need to reform it.[86] Schechter has taken up this theme, examining a range of radical, democratic and socialist alternatives to capitalism.[87] After communism, the paradigm of radical democracy has been regained.

Postcommunism in Perspective

Adam Michnik noted that 'if there is anything worse than communism itself, it is what comes after'.[1] The so-called triumph over communism as an idea and a practice is thoroughly ambiguous: the West ultimately did little to bring about 'victory' in the cold war; the management of international affairs since the end of the cold war remains as arbitrary and confused as before; the postcommunist countries themselves have been afflicted by a growing gulf between the powerful and the powerless and distorted by generalized inequality, and a number of them, a decade after the fall of communism, remained firmly locked in recession; the international system is skewed as seldom before to favour the interests of one particular state and its accolytes; and tensions remain over whether the triumph was that of capitalism or some substantive vision of democracy. While it becomes increasingly clear 'who won' at communism's demise, the answer to 'what won' is less clear-cut.

Politics after communism – the death of the alternative?

The postcommunist transition is, if nothing else, discursively constructed as choiceless, undermining the return of politics as the mobilization of alternatives and weakening the quality of the new democracies. The logic of choicelessness was particularly marked during *perestroika*, reflected in the well-known collection of essays edited by Yurii Afanas'ev, *Inogo ne dano* (*There Is No Choice*).[2] Postcommunism is stamped by a similar implacable logic, reinforced by the teleology of transition itself. The study of postcommunist societies is marked by a dualism where the examination of what actually exists is tempered by an awareness of the potential for the emergence of something else. Even if the existing state of affairs is 'transitional' to some form of capitalist democratic state, the question of what sort of market system, and what sort of democracy, remains. The division between 'is' and 'ought' (*Sein und Sollen*), indeed, is not transcended, but even Georg Lukács insisted on the ultimate autonomy of 'decisions between alternatives'.[3] Kolakowski famously suggested that one of the central features of Stalinism was the 'blackmail of the single alternative in political life'.[4] Postcommunism might well have signalled the return of politics, but this too often appeared to be a politics bereft of what the ancient Greeks considered made politics worthwhile, isonomy (equality of political rights) and autonomy.

But are there alternatives, and what political forms can they take? Havel notoriously asserted that the Third Path leads to the Third World, while others insist that the First Path, so choicelessly propounded by international financial organizations (IFOs), leads to the Fourth World, a peculiar combination of deindustrialization, corruption, criminalization, mass immiseration and comprador capitalism. Havel's condemnation of the application of the term 'postcommunist' to the region stressed that these countries are not defined by their communist pasts alone, and his call for the 'common creation of a new order in European and Euro-Asian affairs' affirmed that the West alone should not determine the shape of the post-cold war order.[5] The demise of revolutionism was accompanied by the marginalization of the discourse of protest and the paralysis of traditional vehicles for popular movements, trade unions and parties, while the very language of justice became disoriented. For Lyotard, the grand modernist metatheories of truth or justice were no more than language games; the appeal to objective truth was replaced by narratives. The exhaustion of utopianism deprived political movements of a heavenly standard against which to judge earthly reality. 'Living without an alternative', deprives current reality of the thrill of critique and anticipation.

The setting up of a series of simple binary oppositions – East versus West, totalitarianism versus democracy, civilization versus barbarism – closed down possibilities of a third option. As the editor of a four-volume Russian collection of articles entitled *Inoe* (*The Other*), a direct challenge to Afanas'ev's volume *Inogo ne dano*, suggested, humanity cannot live by such simple oppositions.[6]

Few of the substantive criticisms made by the revolutionary socialist challenge to capitalist modernity have yet been resolved.
Perhaps more importantly, few of the pathological abnormalities of
modern society identified by Durkheim have yet been transcended.
The fact that the twentieth-century revolutionary socialist challenge in its Leninist guise was despicably crude, failing to engage
with the greater part of Marx's own emancipatory impulse let alone
with the substantial critiques advanced by the likes of Durkheim
and Weber, disguises the fundamental problem that overcoming
the Leninist legacy is only part of placing these societies back on
the path of healthy 'normal' development, to use Durkheim's language. The transcendence of communism does not denote the resolution of the problems that had given rise to it in the first place.

The cold war represented a period of political glaciation when
democratic development itself entered a period of stagnation.
While the formal options were broad, in practice the choices available to democratic electorates were limited. The postcommunist
thaw, however, has not noticeably increased the range and depth of
political choice and debate. Post-colonial states at least had the
choice of taking a socialist-oriented path or an unequivocally capitalist one; postcommunist societies appear faced by a fundamental
choicelessness, and this indeed appears to be one of postcommunism's defining features. The key ingredient of politics is the
existence of a viable political option. Max Weber called this 'an
acceptable alternative', but the choices after 1989–91, it appeared,
were predetermined, whether by social factors (élite transformation) or politically ('the return to Europe').

The gulf between formal and substantive democracy is in most
places the defining feature of postcommunist democratization. If
modernity is characterized by the gradual extension of the legitimate sphere of political action, postcommunism represents the dramatic collapse, and indeed retreat, of the political, defined here as
the sphere in which purposive political agency can legitimately
claim to change 'the reality of things'. The Jacobins and the Bolsheviks shared a common aspiration to retrieve the classical notion
of universal and *complete* citizenship in which all could participate
in the exercise of collective sovereignty. Liberalism, however, has
a prepolitical element that 'ring-fences' certain spheres of social
life, limiting popular sovereignty and reaffirming the notion of an
inviolable private sphere. 'Anti-politics' was concerned with the

structure of collective action while insisting that individual decisions of conscience were themselves a type of public political action, but, as we have noted, there was no way to institutionalize this form of public virtue under postcommunism.

If postcommunism is seen as part of the post-industrial syndrome, then it is not surprising that the great social movements associated with industrial society should have declined. As Lash notes, 'it is these newer, post-industrial middle classes, with their bases in the media, higher education, finance, advertising, merchandising and international exchanges, that provide an audience for postmodern culture'.[7] An examination of protest in postcommunist countries reveals the weakening of the traditional language and movements of collective action. This is only the sharpest manifestation of the weakness of classical 'linkage' organizations (trade unions, parties and legislatures) and the decline of the 'new social movements' that had burgeoned in the late *perestroika* years.[8] The great social movements of modernity appear emasculated. State nationalism is marked by its relative weakness, used by various élite groups in factional struggles and by leadership cabals to sustain themselves in power, but on the whole (with certain exceptions, such as former Yugoslavia and western Ukraine) it is not a major social force. Similarly, the workers' movement everywhere is astonishingly weak, especially given the dire economic difficulties facing these societies. The general deterioration in living standards and quality of life has provoked remarkably little protest. In Russia, for example, inequality increased dramatically, with the average wages of the top 10 per cent of the best-paid workers at least 26 times higher than the average wages of the 10 per cent worst-paid, while the incomes of the richest 10 per cent were 13.1 times higher than the incomes of the poorest 10 per cent. By 1998 at least a quarter of the population lived below the poverty line. With a shrinking economic pie, labour leaders fear that militancy might reduce even the few crumbs that remain; labour militancy might be considered a privilege of an expanding economy.

Postcommunism has starkly revealed the relationship between power and knowledge. As Frederic Raphael has argued: 'When power fails, attendant ideas and icons lose their force. How else could we explain the way in which the "charm" of communism and the "need" to take it seriously was dispelled overnight when Soviet power collapsed?'[9] The range over which political ideas can be discussed appears to have narrowed. The West became a type of

spatial utopia in place of the temporal one sought by earlier revolutions. The shift is more than from an axis of time to one of space,
but is also one from thought to physicality, from the consumption
of ideas to the idea of consumption. Intellectuals today are
regarded with the type of suspicion that was once reserved for travellers and players. Abbott Gleason remarks that this attack on
intellectuals, led in the United States by neo-conservative journal-
ists and public intellectuals such as Irving Kristol, Norman Pod-
horetz and the late Robert Nisbet, systematically denigrates 'the
efforts of intellectuals to envisage and work for what they regard
as a better world ... At best, say the neo-conservatives, they are
likely to be useless and utopian – at worst they are the most important agents of totalitarianism'.[10] The twentieth century has provided gruesome witness to the dangers of utopian projects and the
fanatical attempt to implement idealistic visions of a better and
more communal world, but the end of this stream of thought has
given rise to a widespread cynicism.

The ontological bases for collective action appear to have been
eroded. Marxist revolutionism represented one aspect of the
Enlightenment belief that there are no problems of human social
organization that cannot be resolved by the application of reason.
However, as Giddens argues, 'the old Enlightenment belief that
uncertainties were dissolved by the acquisition of knowledge is
increasingly giving way to the realisation that the present production of knowledge *produces* uncertainty'.[11] The great promise of
modernity, that we can know and master our lives and the world we
live in, has proved false. Ulrich Beck, among others, has defined
contemporary challenges in what he calls 'the risk society'.[12] While
many are clear that something has to be done, no one is quite clear
what, and there is naturally concern that action itself might exacer-
bate the problems. Precisely when material and technological
progress makes possible new forms of human community that could
finally bring the entire world into the compass of sustainable
development to achieve the rudiments of social justice, the very
idea of the future, as a programme and an ideal, has dissolved. If
today we were to ask what progress is, then most of us would be
hard put to answer coherently. At the heart of twentieth-century
revolution was the idea of progress, and the ebbing of the revolutionary tide has been accompanied by scepticism towards its
concomitant social progressivism. 'At the end of the century we're

in a very unheroic, unPromethean, unromantic culture', as Michael Ignatieff put it.[13] Postcommunism is in part the politics of paralysis.

Transition and development

The notion of postcommunist transition is composed of four essential elements: overcoming the past; an accelerated period of change before normal evolutionary development is restored; a relatively homogeneous pattern of change between countries; and a teleological element that assumes a known end point. All four of these elements can be criticized. How much of the past can be salvaged, and is not the radical repudiation of the past a characteristic of communism that the societies seek to overcome? It is already clear, moreover, that the modes of extrication from the communist past take as many different forms as there are countries. Finally, while some countries are well on track to achieve the 'normality' prevalent in Western Europe, others are fast-forwarding to the past, with the re-emergence of archaic clan politics accompanied by the traditionalization of society.

While postcommunism has seen the retreat of Marxist historicism, there has been a corresponding rise in liberal historicism. The notion of transition as a logical phase in the development of society from a recognized starting point to a known end point is rooted in the great metanarratives of modernity, of lineal and universal development patterns for all societies. At the heart of the concept of postcommunism is a remedial concept of transition. Communist societies, it is implied, had set out on a path of development that sought to achieve the fruits of modernity but by an alternative path. This experiment, it is then suggested, not only failed but burdened the societies with distorted economies and societies. The task of postcommunism is to overcome these distortions and to set the society back on to the path of democratic capitalist modernity. Lane has argued that the term 'transition' cannot be taken to mean that one outcome is inevitable.[14] As Bunce and Csanadi insist,

> in our view fluidity and uncertainty are *the* fundamental characteristics of the transitional period . . . With so much in transition and thus so much uncertain, the new political formations in Eastern Europe can hardly be understood as regimes in transition to capitalism and liberal democracy. Rather, these are post-communist in nature, and their future is unknown.[15]

The concept of transition is unduly mechanical since the very process of change in individual countries alters the dynamics of the system as a whole. The collection of essays edited by Bryant and Mokrzycki takes up the theme of the open-endedness of historical processes.[16] They insist that it is more appropriate to speak of a transformation, in which only the point of departure is known, than a transition, which assumes a guaranteed end state as the destination. The essays suggest that post-communist systems have themselves become a new social formation marked not only by the legacy of 40 years of Soviet-type rule but also by the neo-utopianism of the 'Bolsheviks of the market', whose policies by and large have predominated since 1989. This, however, begs the question: could the hopes for reconstituting civil society and formalizing political and economic pluralism have been pursued in some other way? The answer, according to Maurice Glasman in this collection, is a resounding yes. In a sophisticated reconstruction and application to Eastern Europe of Karl Polanyi's arguments in *The Great Transformation* on the emergence of the modern market capitalist system,[17] Glasman argues that some combination of social democracy and social markets was a viable alternative, but in seeking to explain why this option, implemented so successfully in West Germany's social market economy, was not adopted he falls back on some rather simplistic reasoning. He insists that 'there is no alternative to the market, but the market is no alternative',[18] but the roots of the neo-liberal utopianism prevalent under postcommunism remain unexplored. While the social democratic project might be attractive, empirical evidence on how social democracy as a political movement has fared in postcommunist Europe reveals a uniformly poor performance.[19]

Postcommunism, like the communism that preceeded it, has to be located in the larger context of state formation and developmental paths. Japan since the Meiji restoration has with justice been defined as a 'developmental state', as well as being 'preservationist' – preserving the spirit if not the form of the past. After 1945, developmentalism became the ideology of post-fascist reconstruction. Chinese communism, too, had a profound developmental current that triumphed under Deng Xiaoping. Elsewhere questions of developmental patterns and paths remain unresolved. The problems faced by Russia at the beginning of the century, for example, have not gone away but have reappeared in new forms today. One of the paradoxes we discussed earlier is the *economism* pervading the postcommunist transitions. Just as Soviet-type socialism had represented its own distinctive polit-economization of the dynamics of political change, today the power of capital appears to be less the accompaniment of modern society than its substitute. While universalistic post-Communism revolts against the idea of historical necessity, practical postcommunism appears to be dominated by a deterministic logic that is as strong as it is opposed in content to the necessitarianism that had become so prevalent in revolutionary socialism. In practice, postcommunist capitalism differs from neoclassical capitalism in little more than its origins. In every country distinctive practices emerged, but in basic forms the laws of capitalism appeared, indeed, global.

The destination of the transitions itself is undergoing a profound transformation. The tension between postcommunism and post-Communism is not easily resolved. The 'normality' to which post-communist societies aspire is far from homogeneous and the 'West' which these countries hope to become has changed. A whole genre of analysis suggests that the 'late' capitalism at the end of the millennium is part of the fragmented economic order of postmodernity in which social analysis based on class exploitation or economic models based on supply and demand cannot even begin to encompass the complexity of globalization.[20] The very notion of 'work' itself, it has been argued, has lost its centrality in the constitution of social and economic identity.[21] This deconstructionist model of contemporary economy can be challenged. Despite the elements of fragmentation and disarticulation, modern capitalism retains a strong developmental model focused on concepts of rationalization and measured in terms of gross national product growth.

When does a transition end? In the political sphere this is usually defined in terms of the consolidation of democracy, one (or possibly two) changes of governments by legal means and the rule of law to which the state itself is subordinate. In economics it is when the essentials of a market system have been introduced: price liberalization and competition; a significant share of output produced by the private sector; privatization and changes in corporate governance; the establishment of an effective banking sector; and openness to world trade. The transition, however, is not synonymous with postcommunism although it overlaps with its early phases. At a certain point the heuristic value of the notion of postcommunism will diminish to the point that we will enter the post-postcommunist era. At this time national cultures and global processes will predominate, although in tension with each other, but other than this, the philosophical charge of this epoch is unknown. In practical terms, postcommunism ends when the notion of transition is abandoned, but understood as a universal phenomenon postcommunism defines the problem of finding new forms of political articulation in the era of globalization.

The political aesthetics of postcommunism – reshaping subjectivity

It is easy to underestimate the seismic shift in social theory and political context represented by the fall of communism. Not only did an unprecedentedly large number of countries simultaneously embark on fundamental transformations of their polities, economies and international relations, but a whole epoch of social thinking came to a shuddering halt. The strand in Enlightenment thinking that stressed the revolutionary transformation of humanity was amplified by Marx and implemented by Lenin, and at the end of the twentieth century was repudiated not only by those living in the systems but also by most of the rest of the world. For the remaining communist countries the aim was no longer social transformation and human emancipation from class oppression but efficient state management.

The fall of communism has been represented as the collapse of modernity in its entirety, but it could with equal plausibility be taken to represent the vindication of modernity. The great transformative 'metanarratives' of modernity appear to have exhausted themselves, above all revolutionary socialism, yet the power of, say, liberalism and nationalism is by no means discharged. John Gray, too, has taken up the question of quite what has ended with the fall of communism. Not only liberalism and the Enlightenment itself have no future, but the fundamental 'end-game' is the demise of Westernizing universalism, of which neo-liberalism is only the last hurrah. He subjects neo-liberalism to the familiar litany of charges: that unrestrained markets destroy local communities, undermine political sovereignty and political accountability, and are themselves prone to crisis.[22] The critique of Enlightenment thinking is in keeping with the best traditions of the Enlightenment itself, while at the same time it shares the Kantian liberation from the need to anchor that critique in a sustained utopian alternative to the present and thus shares some of the characteristics of the post-communist transcending revolutions themselves.

While endings might preoccupy Western theorists, the problem of continuity vexes the East. A question that is particularly acute in Russia and China but which is not entirely absent elsewhere is whether communism was only a symptom of a more profound malaise in that particular country's historical trajectory. For many, communism in Russia reflected deeper patterns of social authoritarianism and imperial traditions. If so, then both communism and postcommunism are only aspects of a larger problem reflecting what Staniszkis has called 'cultural ontology', what others earlier called political culture. Jonathan Steele, for example, has sugested that the recurring patterns of authoritarianism in 'eternal Russia' emerge from some deep-rooted characteristics of the country,[23] and what Steele has argued in a tentative and academic manner, others (like Zbigniew Brzezinski) have asserted with greater stridency.

The collapse of the communist state ideology was accompanied by the erosion of its social norms. The egalitarian social principles of the Soviet period were denigrated on the grounds that they inhibited the development of market relations. Super-rich strata emerged that sought to consolidate their positions by colonizing the new political systems and marginalizing broader social groups. In some countries the relatively successful switch to a market economy and location close to the Western European prosperity zone saw a general improvement in the conditions of the mass of the population, or at least allowed most to feel that improvement would be not long in coming. But for those further out in the periphery the desocialization of the economy, the destruction of welfare systems and the erosion of political responsiveness gave rise to the political marginalization and the impoverishment of large sections of society. Postcommunist mass publics lacked both ideological and organizational resources to influence their own governments, let alone transnational agencies that were shaping their future.

Postcommunism was accompanied by a crisis of political aesthetics. It is no longer *bon ton* to be politically engaged, the struggle against evils like land-mines is left to royalty, and capitalism becomes a matter of style rather than exploitation. The figure of the

nonconformist and the eccentric is tolerated less than at any time
before, and failures are treated as personal inadequacies rather
than elements of a broader systemic fault. An ethical revolution has
taken place, denigrating altruism and service for the common good
in favour of a new type of 'holy selfishness'. Gleason puts it as
follows: 'purposive self-aggrandisement is regarded as not only
normal but in some sense as defining moral activity. Selfishness is
highly respectable and even mild egalitarianism in regarded with
suspicion.'[24]

The left in this context has lost its role as the custodian of the
future. The economic case for socialism is no longer as compelling
as it once might have been, and in its place moral and cultural arguments come to the fore. Merquior's argument in his *Western
Marxism* has been summarized as follows:

> Disappointed with the totalitarian inflexion of Soviet socialism, West-
> ern Marxists in Germany and France abandoned their obsessive criti-
> cism of the democratic format of liberal economies, to concentrate on
> the cultural criticism of the productivism and technism of bourgeois
> society. Perry Anderson's verdict is incisive and correct: Western
> Marxism adopts 'method as powerlessness, art as consolation, and
> pessimism as quiescence'.[25]

A similar point was made by Fred Inglis who notes: 'The death of
socialism, at least in Europe, happened all at once and, thanks to
Gorbachev, without bloodshed. It caught the intelligentsia of the
left unprepared. It made them bereft.'[26] The god of revolutionary
socialism may well have failed, but the response need not be a postmodern despair: there is still plenty enough evil in the world to be
combated and human potential to be realized. Instead, Inglis continues, the intellectual left, that has grown into a substantial status
group as a result of the expansion of higher education, 'powerlessly
stud[ies] power, lacking capital of its own, bad at economic theory,
fired by fine ideals. These are the curates of utopia, the reporters of
the news from nowhere'.[27]

In postcommunist societies the dilemma of nonconformity is particularly acute: 'Paradoxically, the luxury of freedom has created as
many problems as it solved, sweeping away the hero status of the
nonconformist, often revealing works whose only prior achievement was its very existence'.[28] A similar point was made by the
Czech writer, Eva Klímová: 'Before, nothing was allowed and

everything seemed important. Now everything is allowed and nothing seems important'.[29] If Solzhenitsyn had characterized writers under communism as 'a second government', whose persecution for heterodoxy was itself a form of homage, postcommunism represented a more fundamental assault against the status of the intellectual. The hero of the new age was the entrepreneur, while artists lost their privileges and had to find a new role in a commercial environment. The collapse in 1989–91 respresented the dissolution not only of a modernistic political order but also of Western Europe's own past, a society permeated by the high-mindedness and seriousness about ideas that had long ago been eroded in the West. For Jean Baudrillard, '[t]he iron curtain was drawn to reveal an insatiable appetite for simulation'.[30]

Havel's resolution of the problem of the self in the new society was the development of a new 'subjecthood', the rehabilitation of 'our sense of ourselves as active human subjects'.[31] For Foucault the development of modernity was associated with the shaping of a specific subjectivity, and so, too, the postcommunist individual is faced with the challenge of rapidly acquiring a subjectivity that had taken centuries to evolve in the West. This is the problem facing all rapidly modernizing societies, and while Huntington take a macro-cultural approach to the issue, it is in the micro-world of changed understanding of the world around us that the most fundamental and durable changes take place.

Postcommunism and the future – a postcommunist manifesto?

Postcommunism is both a movement and an ideal. The formulation of the aim, and how to get there, are the concern of the movement, while as a state of mind postcommunism shares many of the angsts of the *fin de siècle* mentality. Postcommunism is part of a larger group of 'post' philosophies reflecting the uncertainties of our age. The affinities between postcommunism and postmodernity have been suggested above, although the differences should be stressed, focusing above all on the idealist elements. Both assume the end of utopianism, the belief that some complete better state of humanity can be achieved on earth. In this sense we have moved from the age of ideology, launched at the time of the Enlightenment, to a new age of ideas, a more humanistic open-ended view of human development.

While ideas are not lacking in the postcommunist epoch, the notion of *the* idea encompassing all the manifold tendencies of our age is weakened. While communism systemically overestimated the possibilities of politics, postcommunism as a movement fundamentally denigrates the potential for purposive political action. As an ideal, however, the revolutions of 1989–91 not only destroyed most state socialist regimes but opened up perspectives for open social development. The revival of the idiom of the 'third way' acknowledges earlier attempts at post-ideological 'beyond left and right' forms of social development, but it was also a recognition that postcommunist politics required some sort of positive agenda. While globalization limits the scope of governmental action, this does not entail the abnegation of governmental responsibility for social development. A leaner state does not mean no state at all.

It is thus only when viewed in its dual aspect that postcommunism becomes a useful analytical tool. As a movement postcommunism encompasses one of the most grandiose acts of political and economic reconstitution in history. Twenty-seven European countries simultaneously reoriented almost all facets of their social existence, while a number of Asian countries maintained continuity in form yet gradually hollowed out the content of the former social project to which they had been committed. This, of course, is not a movement as an organized agency but as one of those fundamental shifts in history that reorders the accustomed order. To say that these countries, ranging from the baroque splendours of the Czech Republic to the cotton fields of Uzbekistan, have nothing in common except their communist past is to underestimate the impact of the communist experience, even when it became bound up with native traditions. As a movement, of course, postcommunism is temporary and transitional, but as a defined historical period it has unique features that will always be inscribed as 'the postcommunist era'.

As an ideal postcommunism had not only a negative, rejective, logic – namely overcoming the legacy of communism – but also a more positive, inclusive, agenda. This agenda necessarily remains vague in that there is no single postcommunist manifesto broadcasting its aims, but it remains central to our age as an opportunity to achieve certain normative goals: the strengthening of international civil society including those aspects concerned with universal justice; the drive to ensure minimum standards of good governance and human rights; and, perhaps above all, to deepen democracy everywhere while extending the rights associated with the ideal of social citizenship balanced by an acknowledgement of the duties associated with membership in a political community. There is no reason to think that the ideals associated with post-communism will be any more successful than those identified with communism itself – except for the genesis of the concept. By reject-ing the violence and instrumentality of communism, postcom-munism may paradoxically fulfil some of the moral aspirations of revolutionary socialism while rejecting its materialist basis. By returning to the idealist charge that had given birth to Marxian socialism in the first place, postcommunism may, however, surren-der to the economic determinism from which communism sought to emancipate humanity but to which it became itself enthralled.

While postcommunism obviously comes after communism, what comes after postcommunism remains a mystery. How long will the former communist countries be classified as transitional societies? There will come a point when we will be able to say that postcom-munism as a movement is over: the societies concerned will have more or less functioning market economies, their political systems will no longer have their communism as a reference point and their place in the international system will no longer be determined by the past and the attempts to overcome it. The destinations of the postcommunist countries will no doubt vary widely. As an ideal, however, the end point of postcommunism will be less easy to determine. It is unlikely that the 'lessons of history' will be learnt: as Mattick notes, they are usually wasted on the new generation 'which often merely repeats in a more insolent fashion and with less sophistication the proven mistakes of the past'.[32] Yet postcom-munism is not just a negative phenomenon but opens up prospects for social and political renewal. It is this challenge that has yet to be grasped. When there is no longer the attempt to learn from the experience of communism and its transcendence, then we will be able to say that postcommunism is over.

Notes

Chapter 1

1 Eric Hobsbawm, *Age of Extremes: The Short Twentieth Century, 1914–1991* (London: Abacus, 1995).
2 Václav Havel, 'The Post-Communist Nightmare', *The New York Review*, 27 May 1993, p. 10.
3 According to Arpád Szakolczai and Agnes Horváth, 'The Discourse of Civil Society and the Self-elimination of the Party', in Paul Lewis (ed.), *Democracy and Civil Society in Eastern Europe* (New York: St. Martin's Press, 1992), pp. 16–17, 1989 was 'perhaps the first case in which the holders of power simply gave up their position without the existence of an organised, massive opposition to the regime ... In our interpretation, this type of complete loss and internal dissolution can only happen if it is realised that the rationality of the system was dubious from the very start'.
4 Kenneth Jowitt, 'A World Without Leninism', in Jowitt, *New World Disorder: The Leninist Extinction* (Berkeley: University of California Press, 1992), p. 310.
5 Grouped by region the countries are:

- East Central Europe – Poland, Czech Republic, Slovakia, Hungary (and, residually, Eastern Germany, absorbed into the Federal Republic in 1990);
- Balkans – Albania, Bosnia, Bulgaria, Romania, Slovenia, Croatia, Macedonia and the Federal Republic of Yugoslavia (Serbia and Montenegro);
- Baltic – Estonia, Latvia and Lithuania;
- Slavic – Belarus, Ukraine and Russia;
- Moldova;
- South Caucasus – Armenia, Azerbaijan and Georgia;

- Central Asia – Kazakhstan, Kyrgyzstan, Tajikistan, Turkmenistan and Uzbekistan.

If we include Yugoslavia as two separate countries and the former German Democratic Republic, then the number rises to 29. The total, moreover, is likely to rise: Russia already contains a number of proto-states, above all Chechnya; Georgia is struggling to retain Abkhazia and South Ossetia, but Adjaria is quiescent; the Crimean Republic is unlikely to leave Ukraine, but tensions remain; the status of Armenian-populated Nagorno-Karabakh, formally subordinate to Azerbaijan, remains unresolved; and possibly Kosovo will secede from Serbia.

6 Zygmunt Bauman, 'After the Patronage State: A Model in Search of Class Interest', in Christopher Bryant and Edmund Mokrzycki (eds), *The New Great Transformation* (London: Routledge, 1994), pp. 15–19.

7 'Death of centres' and 'incredulity towards metanarratives' is how Paul Dukes, *World Order in History: Russia and the West* (London: Routledge, 1996), p. 184, fn 6, paraphrases Lyotard.

Chapter 2

1 Neil Harding, 'Marx, Engels and the *Manifesto*: Working Class, Party, and the Proletariat', *Journal of Political Ideologies*, vol. 3, no. 1, 1998, p. 35.

2 Karl Marx and Friedrich Engels, 'The German Ideology', in Lewis S. Feuer (ed.), *Marx and Engels: Basic Writings on Politics and Philosophy* (London: Fontana, 1969), p. 298.

3 Edward Bernstein, 'The Theory of Collapse and Colonial Policy', in H. Tudor and J. M. Tudor (eds), *Marxism and Social Democracy: The Revisionist Debate 1896–1898* (Cambridge: Cambridge University Press, 1988), pp. 168–9. Originally published in *Neue Zeit*, 19 January 1898.

4 Paul Mattick, 'Karl Kautsky: From Marx to Hitler' in Paul Mattick, *Anti-Bolshevik Communism* (London: Merlin Press, 1978), p. 3.

5 Donald Sassoon, *One Hundred Years of Socialism: The West European Left in the Twentieth Century* (London: Fontana Press, 1997).

6 See ibid., p. 249.

7 Anthony Crosland, *The Future of Socialism*, 2nd edn (London: Jonathan Cape, 1967).

8 Michael Bakunin, *Statism and Anarchy*, translated and edited by Marshall S. Shatz (Cambridge: Cambridge University Press, 1990), p. 24.

9 Robin Blackburn, 'Socialism after the Crash', in Robin Blackburn (ed.), *After the Fall: The Failure of Communism and the Future of Socialism* (London: Verso, 1991), p. 183.

10 Karl Marx, 'The Civil War in France' (1871), in Feuer, *Marx and Engels*, p. 408.

11 Cf. David W. Lovell, *From Marx to Lenin: An Evaluation of Marx's Responsibility for Soviet Authoritarianism* (Cambridge: Cambridge University Press, 1984), p. 192.
12 See A. J. Polan, *Lenin and the End of Politics* (London: Methuen, 1984).
13 Samuel Farber, *Before Stalinism: The Rise and Fall of Soviet Democracy* (London: Verso, 1990), p. 179.
14 Paul Mattick, 'Luxemburg versus Lenin', in Mattick, *Anti-Bolshevik Communism*, p. 32.
15 Rosa Luxemburg, *The Russian Revolution and Leninism or Marxism?* (Ann Arbor: University of Michigan Press, 1961), p. 68.
16 Karl Kautsky, *The Dictatorship of the Proletariat* (Ann Arbor: University of Michigan Press, 1964), pp. 6–7, 47.
17 Stephen Cohen, *Bukharin and the Bolshevik Revolution: A Political Biography, 1888–1938* (New York: Vintage, 1975).
18 Boris Nicolaevsky, *Power and the Soviet Elite* (New York: Praeger, 1965), p. 13.
19 *The Action Programme of the Czechoslovak Communist Party. Prague, April 1968* (Nottingham: Spokesman Books, 1970).
20 The landmark Western formulation of the problem is Andrew Arato, 'Civil Society against the State: Poland 1980–81', *Telos*, no. 47, 1981, pp. 23–47. Michnik's own theorization of the strategy of social 'self-defence' and 'passive revolution' (even though he does not use the term), is Adam Michnik, 'A New Evolutionism', in Michnik, *Letters from Prison and other Essays* (Berkeley: University of California Press, 1985), pp. 135–48.
21 The best-known, although sketchily developed, statement of the case is Georgi Konrad, *Antipolitics* (London: Quartet, 1984).
22 See, in particular, J.A. Cohen and A. Arato, *Civil Society and Political Theory* (Cambridge, MA: MIT Press, 1992); John Keane (ed.), *Civil Society and the State: New European Perspectives* (London: Verso, 1988); John Keane (ed.), *Democracy and Civil Society* (London: Verso, 1988).
23 L. Nowak, *Power and Civil Society: Towards a Dynamic Theory of Real Socialism* (Westport, CT: Greenwood Press, 1991), p. 57.
24 Paul Heywood, 'Introduction: of Chance, and Death, and Mutability', in Martin J. Bull and Paul Heywood (eds), *West European Communist Parties after the Revolutions of 1989* (London: Macmillan, 1994), p. xviii. See also Fernando Claudin, *The Democratic Road to Socialism* (London: New Left Books, 1978), pp. 65–6.
25 A. Tsipko, 'Istoki Stalinizma', *Nauka i zhizn'*, no. 11, 1988, pp. 45–55; no. 12, 1988, pp. 40–55; no. 1, 1989, pp. 46–56; no. 2, 1989, pp. 53–61.
26 M.S. Gorbachev, *Perestroika: New Thinking for Our Country and the World* (London: Collins, 1987).
27 See, for example, Igor Belikov, 'Soviet Scholars' Debate on Socialist Orientation in the Third World', *Millenium*, vol. 20, no. 1, 1991, pp.

23–40; Jerry F. Hough, *The Struggle for the Third World* (Washington, DC: Brookings, 1986).

28 Yegor Ligachev, *Inside Gorbachev's Kremlin* (Boulder, CO: Westview Press, 1996), p. 134.

29 For an interpretation of *perestroika* in this light, see Richard Sakwa, 'Commune Democracy and Gorbachev's Reforms', *Political Studies*, vol. 37, no. 2, 1989, pp. 224–43.

30 Gorbachev, *Perestroika*, pp. 49–59.

Chapter 3

1 Letter to Vera Zasulich, 23 April 1885, quoted in R.V. Daniels, *The End of the Communist Revolution* (London: Routledge, 1993), p. 101.

2 George Schöpflin, 'The End of Communism in Eastern Europe', *International Affairs*, vol. 66, no. 1, 1990, p. 3.

3 Daniels, *The End of the Communist Revolution*, pp. 98–116.

4 Neil Harding, 'The Marxist-Leninist Detour', in John Dunn (ed.), *Democracy: The Unfinished Journey, 508 BC to AD 1993* (Oxford: Oxford University Press, 1993), pp 155–88.

5 *The Guardian*, 15 December 1989.

6 Robin Blackburn, 'Socialism after the Crash', in Robin Blackburn (ed.), *After the Fall: The Failure of Communism and the Future of Socialism* (London: Verso, 1991), p. 219.

7 Donald Sassoon, *One Hundred Years of Socialism: The West European Left in the Twentieth Century* (London: Fontana Press, 1997), p. 197.

8 Alec Nove, *The Economics of Feasible Socialism* (London: George Allen & Unwin, 1983).

9 Jack Gray, 'Rethinking Chinese Economic Reform', *Journal of Communist Studies and Transition Politics*, vol. 14, no. 3, 1998, pp. 145–6.

10 Merle Fainsod, *Smolensk under Soviet Rule* (London: Macmillan, 1958), pp. 449–51.

11 Katherine Verdery, *What Was Socialism, and What Comes Next?* (Princeton, NJ: Princeton University Press, 1996).

12 Grzegorz Ekiert, *The State against Society: Political Crises and their Aftermath in East Central Europe* (Princeton, NJ: Princeton University Press, 1996), p. 266.

13 Leslie Holmes, *Post-Communism: An Introduction* (Cambridge: Polity Press, 1997), p. 44.

14 Harry Eckstein, Frederic J. Fleron Jr, Erik P. Hoffmann and William M. Reissinger, *Can Democracy Take Root in Post-Soviet Russia? Explorations in State-Society Relations* (Lanham, MD: Rowman & Littlefield, 1998), p. 4.

15 See Philip G. Roeder, *Red Sunset: The Failure of Soviet Politics* (Princeton, NJ: Princeton University Press, 1993).

16 Stephen E. Hanson, *Time and Revolution: Marxism and the Design of Soviet Institutions* (Chapel Hill: University of North Carolina Press, 1997).
17 Timothy Garton Ash, 'Refolution in Hungary and Poland', *New York Review*, 17 August 1989, pp. 9–15; see also Timothy Garton Ash, 'Reform or Revolution?', *New York Review*, 27 October 1988, pp. 47–55.
18 Jürgen Habermas, 'What Does Socialism Mean Today? The Rectifying Revolution and the Need for New Thinking on the Left', *New Left Review*, no. 183, 1990, pp. 3–21.
19 Cf. Leslie Holmes, *The End of Communist Power: Anti-Corruption Campaigns and Legitimation Crisis* (Cambridge: Polity Press, 1993).
20 Klaus von Beyme, *Transition to Democracy in Eastern Europe* (London: Macmillan, 1996), p. 14.
21 Jadwiga Staniszkis, *The Dynamics of Breakthrough in Eastern Europe: The Polish Experience* (Berkeley: University of California Press, 1991).
22 Partisans of the 'revolution from above' scenario include Jerry F. Hough, *Democratization and Revolution in the USSR, 1985–1991* (Washington DC: Brookings Institution Press, 1997), who talks in terms of a 'middle class revolution', and David Kotz with Fred Weir, *Revolution from Above: the Demise of the Soviet System* (London: Routledge, 1997).

Chapter 4

1 Valerie Bunce and Mária Csanádi, 'Uncertainty in the Transition: Post-Communism in Hungary', *East European Politics and Societies*, vol. 7, no. 2, 1993, pp. 246–7.
2 Kenneth Jowitt, 'The Leninist Legacy', in Kenneth Jowitt, *New World Disorder: The Leninist Extinction* (Berkeley: University of California Press, 1992), p. 293.
3 For details, see Karen Henderson and Neil Robinson, *Post-Communist Politics: An Introduction* (Hemel Hempstead: Prentice Hall, 1997).
4 For Samuel P. Huntington, *The Third Wave: Democratization in the Late Twentieth Century* (Norman and London: University of Oklahoma Press, 1991), the first wave lasted from 1776 to 1922, the second from 1945 to the 1960s, and the third began in Southern Europe in 1974 (Portugal) before moving to Latin America and then returning to Eastern Europe in 1989.
5 Juan J. Linz and Alfred Stepan, *Problems of Democratic Transition and Consolidation: Southern Europe, South America, and Post-Communist Europe* (Baltimore, MD: Johns Hopkins University Press, 1996), Chapter 20, pp. 401–33.
6 Valerie Bunce, 'Should Transitologists be Grounded?', *Slavic Review*, vol. 54, no. 1, 1995, p. 119.

7 Grzegorz Ekiert, *The State against Society: Political Crises and their Aftermath in East Central Europe* (Princeton, NJ: Princeton University Press, 1996), p. xiii.
8 Claus Offe, 'Capitalism by Democratic Design? Democratic Theory Facing the Triple Transition in East Central Europe', *Social Research*, vol. 58, no. 4, pp. 865–92.
9 T.H. Rigby, 'Stalinism and mono-organizational society', *The Changing Soviet System* (Aldershot: Edward Elgar, 1990) pp. 88–9.
10 Grzegorz Ekiert, 'Peculiarities of Post-Communist Politics: The Case of Poland', *Studies in Comparative Communism*, vol. 25, pp. 341–61.
11 Ralf Dahrendorf, *Reflections on the Revolution in Europe* (London: Chatto & Windus, 1990), pp. 71–108.
12 John Williamson, *The Political Economy of Policy Reform* (Washington, DC: Institute for International Economics, 1994), pp. 17, 20–28.
13 Kazimierz Poznanski, *Poland's Protracted Transition* (Cambridge: Cambridge University Press, 1998).
14 Leszek Balcerowicz, *Socialism, Capitalism, Transformation* (Budapest: Central European University Press, 1995).
15 Wing Thye Woo, Stephen Parker and Jeffrey D. Sachs (eds), *Economies in Transition: Comparing Asia and Eastern Europe* (Cambridge, MA: MIT Press, 1997), p. 258.
16 Zbigniew Brzezinski, *The Grand Failure: The Birth and Death of Communism in the Twentieth Century* (London: Macdonald, 1989), pp. 1–2.
17 Joseph R. Blasi, Maya Kroumova and Douglas Kruse, *Kremlin Capitalism: Privatizing the Russian Economy* (Ithaca, NY: ILR Press/Cornell University Press, 1997), p. 187.
18 Bartlomiej Kaminski (ed.), *Economic Transition in Russia and the New States of Eurasia* (Armonk, NY: M.E. Sharpe, 1996).
19 Jowitt, 'The Leninist Legacy', p. 294.
20 Jerzy Szacki, *Liberalism after Communism* (Budapest: Central European University Press, 1995).
21 See Adam Przeworski, *Democracy and the Market: Political and Economic Reforms in Eastern Europe and Latin America* (Cambridge: Cambridge University Press, 1991).
22 Jon Elster, 'The Role of Institutional Interest in East European Constitution Making', *East European Constitutional Review*, vol. 5, no. 1, 1996, pp. 63–6.
23 See Karen Dawisha, *Post-Communism's Troubled Steps toward Democracy: An Aggregate Analysis of Progress in the 27 States* (Center for the Study of Post-Communist Societies, University of Maryland, 1997).
24 Linz and Stepan, *Problems of Democratic Transition and Consolidation*, pp. 51–4, 70–1.
25 World Bank, *The East Asian Miracle: Economic Growth and Public Policy* (Oxford: Oxford University Press, 1993).

26 Robert H. Jackson, *Quasi-states: Sovereignty, International Relations and the Third World* (Cambridge: Cambridge University Press, 1991).

27 Abbott Gleason, 'Reinterpreting the Soviet Experience: Phase I', *Newsnet: The Newsletter of the AASS*, vol. 37, no. 1, 1997, p. 2.

28 Václav Havel, *The Art of the Impossible: Politics as Morality in Practice* (New York: Alfred A. Knopf, 1997).

29 Ernest Gellner, *Conditions of Liberty: Civil Society and its Rivals* (London: Hamish Hamilton, 1994), p. 186.

30 Carlton J. Hayes, *The Historical Evolution of Modern Nationalism* (London: Macmillan, 1949), Chapter VI.

31 Tom Nairn, *The Break-up of Britain* (London: New Left Books, 1977), p. 359.

32 Ernest Gellner, *Nations and Nationalism: New Perspectives on the Past* (Oxford: Basil Blackwell, 1983).

33 Anthony D. Smith, *Theories of Nationalism* (London: Duckworth, 1983); see also Anthony D. Smith, *National Identity* (London: Penguin, 1991).

34 Mancur Olson, 'The Logic of Collective Action in Soviet-type Societies', *Journal of Soviet Nationalities*, no. 1, 1990, pp. 23–4.

35 Ibid., pp. 25–6.

36 Rogers Brubaker, 'Nationhood and the National Question in the Soviet Union and Post-Soviet Eurasia: An Institutionalist Account', *Theory and Society*, vol. 23, 1994, pp. 47–78; Rogers Brubaker, *Nationalism Reframed: Nationhood and the National Question in the New Europe* (Cambridge: Cambridge University Press, 1996).

37 Hayes, *The Historical Evolution of Modern Nationalism*, p. 244.

38 Fareed Zakaria, 'The Rise of Illiberal Democracy', *Foreign Affairs*, vol. 76, no. 6, 1997, p. 35.

39 Michael Doyle, *Ways of War and Peace: Realism, Liberalism and Socialism* (New York: Norton, 1997).

40 Zakaria, 'The Rise of Illiberal Democracy', p. 38, drawing on data from work by Jack Snyder and Edward Mansfield demonstrating that over the last 200 years 'democratizing states went to war significantly more often than either stable autocracies or liberal democracies'.

41 Robert Cooper, *The Post-Modern State and the World Order* (London: Demos, 1996), p. 7.

42 See Iver B. Neumann, *Russia and the Idea of Europe: A Study in Identity and International Relations* (London: Routledge, 1996).

43 Hermann Giliomee, 'Democratization in South Africa', *Political Science Quarterly*, vol. 110, no. 1, 1995, pp. 83–104.

44 Adrian Guelke, 'The Impact of the End of the Cold War on the South African Transition', *Journal of Contemporary African Studies*, vol. 14, no. 1 (1996), p. 95.

45 Francis Fukuyama, 'The Next South Africa', *South Africa International*,

October 1991, p. 80, cited by Guelke, 'The Impact of the End of the Cold War', p. 95.

46 Václav Havel, 'A Call for Sacrifice: The Co-responsibility of the West', *Foreign Affairs*, vol. 73, no. 2, 1994, pp. 2, 3 (emphasis added).

47 Jowitt, *New World Disorder*, in particular Chapters 7–9.

48 Hafeez Malik (ed.), *The Roles of the United States, Russia and China in the New World Order* (New York: St. Martin's Press, 1997), p. 56.

49 Havel, 'A Call for Sacrifice' p. 1.

Chapter 5

1 Roberto Campos, 'Merquior the Liberalist', in Ernest Gellner and César Cansino (eds), *Liberalism in Modern Times: Essays in Honour of José G. Merquior* (Budapest: Central European University Press, 1996), p. 66.

2 Ibid., p. 67.

3 Zbigniew Brzezinski, *The Grand Failure: The Birth and Death of Communism in the Twentieth Century* (London: Macdonald, 1989), p. 1.

4 Cited by Agnes Horváth and Arpád Szakolczai, *The Dissolution of Communist Power: The Case of Hungary* (London: Routledge, 1992), p. 8.

5 David Caute, *The Fellow Travellers* (New Haven, CT: Yale University Press, 1988).

6 Stéphane Courtois, 'Les Crimes du Communisme', in Stéphane Courtois (ed.), *Le Livre Noir du Communisme: Crimes, Terreur et Repression* (Paris: Robert Laffont, 1997), pp. 28–33.

7 Cited by Timothy Garton Ash in his review of *Le Livre Noir du Communisme*, *Prospect*, June 1998, p. 66.

8 Courtois, 'Les Crimes du Communisme', p. 14.

9 Ibid., p. 13.

10 Ibid., p. 19.

11 Richard Sakwa, *Soviet Politics: An Introduction* (London: Routledge, 1989), p. 274.

12 Cited by Jean-Louis Margolin, 'Communismes d'Asie: entre "Rééducation" et Massacre', in Courtois (ed.), *Le Livre Noir du Communisme*, p. 545.

13 See Martin Broszat and Saul Friedlander, 'A Controversy about the Historicisation of National Socialism', in Peter Baldwin (ed.), *Reworking the Past: Hitler, the Holocaust and the Historians' Debate* (Boston: Beacon Press, 1990), pp. 1–45.

14 Courtois, 'Les Crimes du Communisme', p. 25.

15 Ibid., p. 33.

16 *Soviet Weekly*, 10 October 1991, p. 6.

17 *Spor o PRL [Controversy over the PRL]* (Cracow: Znak, 1996), a collection of 16 essays.

18 Jakub Karpinski, 'On Stalinist Writings', *Transition*, 10 January 1997, pp. 17–18.
19 Ibid., p. 19.
20 Adam Michnik, 'An Embarrassing Anniversary', *New York Review*, 10 June 1993, p. 19.
21 Alexander Solzhenitsyn, *Stories and Prose Poems* (London: Penguin, 1973), pp. 48–103.
22 Alexander Solzhenitsyn, 'Repentance and Self-Limitation in the Life of Nations', in Alexander Solzhenitsyn (ed.), *From Under the Rubble* (London: Fontana, 1975), pp. 105–43.
23 Jan Jerschina, 'The Catholic Church, the Communist State and the Polish People', in Stanislaw Gomulka and Antony Polonsky (eds), *Polish Paradoxes* (London: Routledge, 1990), p. 83.
24 John Kautsky, *Communism and the Politics of Development* (New York: Wiley, 1968).
25 Excluding the 10,000–15,000 executed, mostly without trial, by the partisans in Italy, or the equal (if not greater) number killed by the resistance during the *épuration* in France.
26 'We are crossing out the past with a thick line. We will only be responsible for what we do in order to get Poland out of the present state of collapse': BBC Monitoring, *Summary of World Broadcasts: Eastern Europe*, 26 August 1989.
27 John Borneman, *Settling Accounts: Violence, Justice, and Accountability in Postsocialist Europe* (Princeton, NJ: Princeton University Press, 1997).
28 Istvan Pogany, *Righting Wrongs in Eastern Europe* (Manchester: Manchester University Press, 1998).
29 For details, see Tina Rosenberg, 'Overcoming the Legacies of Dictatorship', *Foreign Affairs*, vol. 74, no. 3, 1995, pp. 134–52.
30 For a full examination of the dilemmas associated with attempts to bring to justice those guilty of abuses in previous regimes in both communist and non-communist transitions since the Second World War, see Neil J. Kritz (ed.), *Transitional Justice: How Emerging Democracies Reckon with Former Regimes*, 3 vols (Washington, DC: United States Institute of Peace Press, 1995).
31 *RFE/RL Newsline*, 24 June 1998.
32 *RFE/RL Newsline*, 18 June 1998.
33 *Nezavisimaya gazeta*, 9 December 1997.
34 *Rzeczpospolita*, 14 May 1998, cited in *RFE/RL Newsline*, 14 May 1998.
35 *RFE/RL Newsline*, 19 June 1998.
36 Richard Rose, 'Ex-Communists in Post-Communist Societies', *Political Quarterly*, vol. 67, no. 1, 1996, p. 18.
37 Maurizio Cotta, 'Structuring the New Party Systems', in G. Pridham and P. G. Lewis (eds), *Stabilising Fragile Democracies* (London: Routledge, 1996), p. 90.

38 Arpád Szakolczai and Laszlo Fustos, 'Changing Values Leave Ex-Communists Behind', *Transition*, 1 November 1996, p. 48.
39 Jeremy Lester, 'Overdosing on Nationalism', *New Left Review*, no. 221, 1997, p. 37.
40 See Nina Fishman, 'The British Road is Resurfaced for New Times: From the British Communist Party to the Democratic Left', in Martin J. Bull and Paul Heywood (eds), *West European Communist Parties after the Revolutions of 1989*, (London: Macmillan, 1994), pp. 145–77.
41 Robert Hue, 'Communisme aujord'hui: le choix de la personne humaine', *L'Humanité*, 24 February 1998.
42 Yegor Ligachev, *Inside Gorbachev's Kremlin* (Boulder, CO: Westview Press, 1996) p. 378.
43 Poll conducted by Sofres-Factum, *RFE/RL Newsline*, 25 February 1998.

Chapter 6

1 Václav Havel, 'The Post-Communist Nightmare', *The New York Review*, 27 May 1993, p. 8.
2 Immanuel Kant, *Political Writings*, edited and with an introduction and notes by Hans Reiss (Cambridge: Cambridge University Press, 1970), p. 59.
3 For a contrary view, which suggests that even the apparently most anti-Enlightenment revolution of them all, the Iranian revolution, in practice adopted European themes, see Ervand Abrahamian, *Khomeinism* (London: I.B. Tauris, 1994).
4 Andrew Arato, 'Interpreting 1989', *Social Research*, vol. 60, no. 3, 1993, p. 611.
5 John Gray *Post-Liberalism: Studies in Political Thought* (London: Routledge, 1993), pp. 194–5, notes that '[i]t is in the common origins in the secular faith of the Enlightenment that the affinity of the two revolutions [the French and the Russian] is most plainly seen', including such notions as 'a self-consciously planned society' and of 'a universal civilization grounded in scientific knowledge'.
6 Reinhart Koselleck, *Critique and Crisis: Enlightenment and the Pathogenesis of Modern Society* (Oxford: Berg, 1988).
7 Contrary to the common view of Rousseau as the ideologue of the French revolution, Koselleck notes, paradoxically, that Rousseau frequently warned of the dangers 'because the evils of a revolution were greater than the evils it wished to eradicate'; see ibid., p. 161, fn 7. Rousseau thus emerges as the first great anti-revolutionary, insisting on the unity of morality and politics.
8 Cf. Anthony Giddens, *The Consequences of Modernity* (Cambridge: Polity Press, 1990).

9 The characterization is by Eric Voegelin, *From Enlightenment to Revolution* (Durham, NC: Duke University Press, 1975), p. 167.

10 Andrzej Walicki, *Marxism and the Leap to the Kingdom of Freedom: The Rise and Fall of the Communist Utopia* (Stanford, CA: Stanford University Press, 1995).

11 The concept is discussed by Krishan Kumar (ed.), *Revolution: The Theory and Practice of a European Idea* (London: Weidenfeld and Nicolson, 1971), p. 2.

12 Joseph de Maistre, 'Supposed Dangers of Counter-revolution', in *Considerations on France* (Cambridge: Cambridge University Press, 1994), pp. 83–105, at p. 105.

13 Agnes Horváth and Arpád Szakolczai, *The Dissolution of Communist Power: The Case of Hungary* (London: Routledge, 1992); Dmitrii Furman, 'Revolyutsionnye tsikly Rossii', *Svobodnaya mysl'*, no. 1, 1994, p. 9, notes also how the Soviet regime consistently sapped the viability of its own ideology by suppressing all sources of internal renewal.

14 Cf. Ronald Inglehart, *The Silent Revolution* (Princeton, NJ: Princeton University Press, 1977).

15 Timothy Garton Ash, 'Does Central Europe Exist?', in G. Schopflin and N. Wood (eds), *In Search of Central Europe* (Oxford: Polity Press, 1989), pp. 200–1.

16 Theda Skocpol, *Social Revolutions in the Modern World* (Cambridge: Cambridge University Press, 1994), p. 203.

17 For a good study, see Lena Kolarska-Bobinska, 'The Myth of the Market and the Reality of Reform', in Stanislaw Gomulka and Antony Polonsky (eds), *Polish Paradoxes* (London: Routledge, 1990), pp. 160–79.

18 Václav Klaus, *Renaissance: The Rebirth of Liberty in the Heart of Europe* (Washington, DC: Cato Institute, 1997).

19 For example, Karol Modzelewski, *Dokąd od kommunizmu?* [*From Communism to Where?*] (Warsaw: BGW, 1996).

20 Günter Grass, 'Germany after Unification', *Debatte: Review of Contemporary German Affairs*, vol. 5, no. 1, 1997, p. 21.

21 Gabriel Kolko, *Vietnam: Anatomy of a War* (London: Unwin, 1987), Postscript.

22 Gabriel Kolko, *Vietnam: Anatomy of a Peace* (London: Routledge, 1997), Epilogue, pp. 161–8, esp. p. 166.

23 Donald Sassoon, *One Hundred Years of Socialism: The West European Left in the Twentieth Century* (London: Fontana Press, 1997), p. 246.

24 Martin Malia, 'Leninist Endgame', *Daedalus*, vol. 121, no. 2, 1992, p. 70.

25 Daniel Bell, *The Coming of Post-Industrial Society* (New York: Basic Books, 1976), p. xiii.

26 See Robert Skidelsky, *The World after Communism: A Polemic for our Times* (London: Macmillan, 1995).

27 Joseph E. Stiglitz, *Wither Socialism* (Cambridge, MA: MIT Press, 1994).

28 Lester C. Thurow, *The Future of Capitalism* (New York: William Morrow, 1996).

29 James D. White, *Karl Marx and the Intellectual Origins of Dialectical Materialism* (Basingstoke: Macmillan, 1996), p. 56.

30 Jürgen Habermas, 'What Does Socialism Mean Today? The Rectifying Revolution and the Need for New Thinking on the Left', *New Left Review*, no. 183, 1990, p. 5.

31 François Furet, *Le Passé d'une illusion: Essai sur l'idée communiste au XXe siècle* (Paris: Robert Laffont/Calmann-Lévy, 1995), p. 13.

32 Krishan Kumar, 'The Revolutions of 1989: Socialism, Capitalism and Democracy', *Theory and Society*, vol. 21, no. 3, 1992, p. 309.

33 Francis Fukuyama, 'The End of History?', *The National Interest*, Summer 1989, pp. 4, 6; the argument was later developed in Francis Fukuyama, *The End of History and the Last Man* (London: Penguin, 1992).

34 Francis Fukuyama, 'The End of History?', *The National Interest*, Summer 1989, pp. 4, 6.

35 Ibid., p. 8.

36 Stephen Holmes, 'In Search of New Enmities', *London Review of Books*, 24 April 1997, p. 3.

37 Samuel Huntington, *The Clash of Civilizations and the Remaking of World Order* (New York: Simon & Schuster, 1997).

38 Samuel Huntington, 'The West and the Rest', *Prospect*, February 1997, p. 37.

39 Manuel Castells, 'Hauling in the Future', *The Guardian*, 13 December 1997, p. 21.

40 Graham Fuller, 'The Next Ideology', *Foreign Policy*, no. 98, 1995, pp. 152, 154.

41 See Michael Lind, 'Why Intellectual Conservatism Died', *Dissent*, Winter 1995, pp. 42–7. For a developed analysis, see Godfrey Hodgson, *The World Turned Right Side Up: A History of the Conservative Ascendancy in America* (Boston: Houghton Mifflin, 1996).

42 Huntington, 'The West and the Rest', p. 37.

43 'Cultural Revolutions': Stuart Hall in dialogue with Martin Jacques, *New Statesman*, 5 December 1997, p. 24.

44 George Soros, 'The Capitalist Threat', *Atlantic Monthly*, vol. 279, no. 2, 1997, pp. 45–58.

45 Ibid., p. 45.

46 Will Hutton, *The State We're In* (London: Jonathan Cape, 1995), pp. 313–14.

47 For Habermas the legitimation crisis in advanced capitalist states was marked by the increasing inability of the political-administrative system

to manage the economy: see Jürgen Habermas, *Legitimation Crisis* (London: Heineman, 1976), pp. 46–9.

48 Lewis Lapham, 'Goths are at the Gate of Emperor Clinton', *The Guardian*, 27 December 1997, p. 19.

49 André Gorz, *Critique of Economic Reason* (London: Verso, 1989).

50 Richard Rosecrance, 'The Rise of the Virtual State', *Foreign Affairs*, vol. 75, no. 4, 1996, p. 54.

51 Ibid., p. 59.

52 William Greider, *One World, Ready or Not: The Manic Logic of Global Capitalism* (London: Penguin, 1997).

53 Rosecrance, 'The Rise of the Virtual State', p. 60.

54 Viviane Forrester, *L'Horreur Économique* (Paris: Fayard, 1996).

55 P. Hirst and G. Thompson, *Globalization in Question* (Cambridge: Polity Press, 1996), p. 2.

56 Roderick Martin, 'Central and Eastern Europe and the International Economy: The Limits to Globalisation', *Europe-Asia Studies*, vol. 50, no. 1, 1998, p. 9. For a broader analysis of fragmentation, see S. Lash and J. Urry, *The End of Organized Capital* (Cambridge: Polity Press, 1987).

57 Martin, 'Central and Eastern Europe and the International Economy', p. 8.

58 See Peter F. Drucker, 'The Global Economy and the Nation-State', *Foreign Affairs*, vol. 76, no. 5, 1997, p. 167.

59 See Stanley Hoffmann, 'The Crisis of Liberal Internationalism', *Foreign Policy*, no. 98, Spring 1995, p. 175.

60 Ibid.

61 Tom Burke, *New Statesman*, 7 March 1997, p. 47.

62 For example, David Marquand, *The New Reckoning: Capitalism, States and Citizens* (Cambridge: Polity Press, 1997), Chapters 1–3.

63 Robert Reich, *The Work of Nations* (New York: Knopf, 1991).

64 Arthur Lipow, 'Introduction', to Michael Harrington, *Socialism: Past and Future* (London: Pluto Press, 1993), p. vii.

65 Fred Halliday, 'The Ends of Cold War', in Robin Blackburn (ed.), *After the Fall: The Failure of Communism and the Future of Socialism* (London: Verso, 1991), p. 87.

66 Hamish McRae, 'What Awaits Us beyond the Millenium?', *New Statesman*, 20 December 1996, p. 76.

67 Skidelsky, *The World after Communism*, pp. xiii, 17.

68 See Robert Skidelsky, 'The Fall of Keynesianism' and Peter Clarke, 'The Keynesian Consensus and its Enemies', in David Marquand and Anthony Seldon (eds), *The Ideas that Shaped Post-War Britain* (London: Fontana, 1996).

69 Sassoon, *One Hundred Years of Socialism*, p. xxi.

70 Willie Thompson, *The Left in History: Revolution and Reform in Twentieth Century Politics* (London: Pluto, 1997), p. 9.

71 Ibid., p. 231.

72 Norberto Bobbio, *Left and Right: The Significance of a Political Distinction* (Chicago: University of Chicago Press, 1997).

73 This is the argument, at least, of the Italian deputy prime minister, Walter Veltroni, *Governare da Sinistra* (Milan: Baldini and Castaldi, 1997).

74 Martin Jay, *Fin-de-Siècle Socialism and Other Essays* (London: Routledge, 1988).

75 E.P. Thompson, 'A Rejoinder', in Blackburn, *After the Fall*, p. 108.

76 Ibid., p. 108.

77 E.g. A. Callinicos, *The Revenge of History* (Oxford: Polity Press, 1991).

78 R.H. Hudelson, *The Rise and Fall of Communism* (Boulder, CO: Westview Press, 1993), p. 149.

79 On the fate of postcommunist Marxism, see Bernd Magnus and Stephen Cullenberg (eds), *Whither Marxism? Global Crises in International Perspective* (London: Routledge, 1995); and Jacques Derrida, *Specters of Marx: The State of the Debt, The Work of Mourning, and the New International* (London: Routledge, 1994).

80 Istvan Mészáros, *Beyond Capital: Towards a Theory of Transition* (London: Merlin Press, 1995).

81 Ellen Meiksins Wood, *Democracy against Capitalism: Renewing Historical Materialism* (Cambridge: Cambridge University Press, 1995).

82 Habermas, 'What Does Socialism Mean Today?', pp. 19–21.

83 G. Therborn, 'Life and Times of Socialism', *New Left Review*, no. 194, 1992, p. 25.

84 Christopher Pierson, *Socialism after Communism: The New Market Socialism* (Pennsylvania: Pennsylvania University Press, 1995), p. 211.

85 See Anthony Giddens, *The Third Way: The Renewal of Social Democracy* (Cambridge: Polity Press, 1998).

86 E.J. Dionne, *They Only Look Dead: Why Progressives Will Dominate the New Era* (New York: Simon & Schuster, 1996).

87 Darrow Schechter, *Radical Theories* (Manchester: Manchester University Press, 1994).

Chapter 7

1 Recounted to the author by Attila Ágh.

2 Yu.N. Afanas'ev (ed.), *Inogo ne dano* (Moscow: Progress, 1988).

3 Istvan Mészáros, *Lukács' Concept of Dialectic* (London: Merlin Press, 1972), p. 43.

4 Leszek Kolakowski, *Towards a Marxist Humanism* (New York: Grove, 1968), p. 97.

5 Václav Havel, 'A Call for Sacrifice', *Foreign Affairs*, vol. 73, no. 2, 1994, pp. 2–7.

6 S.B. Chernyshev, *Inoe: khrestomatiya novogo Rossiiskogo samosoznaniya*, vol. 4, *Putevoditel'* (Moscow: Argus, 1995), pp. 9–19.

7 S. Lash, *The Sociology of Postmodernism* (London: Sage, 1990), p. 20.
8 For a discussion of these issues in the Polish context, see Grzegorz
   Ekiert, *Public Participation and Politics of Discontent in Post-
   Communist Poland 1989–1992*, Program on Central and Eastern
   Europe, Working Paper Series no. 30, Harvard University, 1993.
9 *New Statesman*, 29 November 1996, p. 38.
10 Abbott Gleason, 'Reinterpreting the Soviet Experience: Phase I',
   Newsnet: The Newsletter of the AASS, vol. 37, no. 1, 1997, p. 1.
11 John Lloyd, 'Interview: Anthony Giddens', *New Statesman*, 10 January
   1997, p. 18.
12 Ulrich Beck, *Risk Society: Towards a New Modernity* (London: Sage,
   1992).
13 *The Independent*, 22 January 1997, p. 18.
14 David Lane (ed.), *Russia in Transition* (Harlow: Longman, 1995), p. xiv.
15 Valerie Bunce and Mária Csanádi, 'Uncertainty in the Transition: Post-
   Communism in Hungary', *East European Politics and Societies*, vol. 7,
   no. 2, 1993, pp. 273, 274.
16 Christopher Bryant and Edmund Mokrzycki (eds), *The New Great
   Transformation* (London: Routledge, 1994).
17 Karl Polanyi, *The Great Transformation* (Boston, MA: Beacon Press,
   1957).
18 Christopher Bryant and Edmund Mokrzycki (eds), *The New Great
   Transformation* (London: Routledge, 1994), p. 213.
19 Michael Waller, Bruno Coppieters and Kris Deschouwer (eds), *Social
   Democracy in a Post-Communist Europe* (London: Frank Cass, 1994).
20 See, in addition to our discussion in Chapter 6, M. Featherstone (ed.),
   Global Culture: Nationalism, Globalisation and Modernity (London:
   Sage, 1990); D. Miller (ed.), *Worlds Apart: Modernity through the Prism
   of the Local* (London: Routledge, 1995).
21 M. Lampland, *The Object of Labor: Commodification in Socialist
   Hungary* (Chicago: University of Chicago Press, 1995).
22 John Gray, *Endgames: Questions in Late Modern Political Thought*
   (Cambridge: Polity Press, 1997).
23 Jonathan Steele, *Eternal Russia* (London: Faber, 1994).
24 Gleason, 'Reinterpreting the Soviet Experience', p. 1.
25 Roberto Campos, 'Merquior the Liberalist', in Ernest Gellner and
   César Cansino (eds), *Liberalism in Modern Times: Essays in Honour of
   José G. Merquior* (Budapest: Central European University Press, 1996),
   p. 73.
26 Fred Inglis, 'Curates of Utopia', *Prospect*, March 1998, p. 71.
27 Ibid.
28 *St Petersburg Times*, 12–19 January 1997.
29 Cited in *Prospect*, November 1997, p. 66.

30 Marina Benjamin in conversation with Jean Baudrillard, *Prospect*, July 1997, p. 19.
31 Václav Havel, 'The Post-Communist Nightmare', *New York Review*, 27 May 1993, p. 10.
32 Paul Mattick, 'Karl Kautsky: From Marx to Hitler', in Paul Mattick, *Anti-Bolshevik Communism* (London: Merlin Press, 1978) p. vii.

Index